EARLY ONE SUNDAY MORNING

I DECIDED TO STEP OUT *and find* SOUTH AFRICA

Luke Alfred

TAFELBERG

Tafelberg
An imprint of NB Publishers a Division of Media24 Boeke (Pty) Ltd
40 Heerengracht, Cape Town
www.tafelberg.com
Text © Luke Alfred (2016)

Cover design: Simon Richardson
Book design: Nazli Jacobs
Editing: Mark Ronan
Proofreading: Sean Fraser
Index: Luke Alfred

Printed and bound by Creda Communications,
Eliot Avenue, Epping II, Cape Town

First edition, first impression 2016

ISBN: 978-0-624-07552-3
Epub: 978-0-624-07553-0
Mobi: 978-0-624-07554-7

To Mom and Dad

CONTENTS

Introduction   9

1   The story of the 'cartridge girls'   11
2   One 'meneer' of a walk   35
3   The many majesties of Thomas Pringle   59
4   Pereira of Paton country   81
5   Fear and loathing on the Fish Hoek
    boardwalk   99
6   Sofasonke City   121
7   'There was no magic about the shorts'   138
8   The man who draped his jacket over
    the Alexandra Dam wall   152
9   A long weekend   169
10 Blue square in the Marico   187
11 The sandalled spectre – a will-o'-the-
    wisp called Gandhi   202
12 The melancholy turnpike: A trample
    along reconciliation's road   218

Acknowledgements   231
Notes and references   233
Index   236

INTRODUCTION

We all walk for different reasons. Charles Dickens rambled at night because of insomnia, getting up the moment he lay down. His walks brought him 'into sympathetic relations with people who have no other object [than to stay awake] every night of the year'. They busied his feet as they opened his soul, curing him of the scourge of wakefulness.

Robert Louis Stevenson and his donkey, Modestine, bashed across the Cévennes to ease Stevenson's love-troubled heart, while Camilo José Cela, the Spanish novelist, walked in the spirit of contrariness. 'The Alcarria is a beautiful region which people apparently have no reason to visit,' he wrote in his picaresque *Journey to the Alcarria*. Then, gently, and at what one might call walking pace, he contradicted himself, charming the region into life in the pages of his wistful book.

I suffer from neither sleeplessness nor a broken heart, so I walk, like Cela, out of curiosity. I wanted to look at South Africa in a different way – from a different angle – and so took to the rhythms of the gravel road, the path and the train track in the hope that such walks would tell me something interesting about my sometimes tortured country. I was tired of the media's white noise. I was distrustful of the soothsayers, the received wisdoms and the platitudes. I come from a family of walkers (Dad was a happy, carefree hiker) and wanted to look at things afresh. The result of taking to the path is this book – a eulogy to South Africa's beauty and the fineness of her people, her indefatigability and the jewel that is her new democracy. It is a book of cautious hope.

Finally, a word on sourcing and fact-checking. I have attempted to verify and second-source my facts wherever possible. In certain cases – the chapter on Modderfontein, for example – this has been exceedingly difficult. My only defence is to point out that this is not an academic study written by a professional historian. Rather, it is a book written by a journalist for a popular audience. For all of its fidelity to the truth, it is also a book full of stories.

Luke Alfred
Kensington, May 2016

1

THE STORY OF THE 'CARTRIDGE GIRLS'

Hope Road, Mountain View, opposite the Victory Theatre, to Modderfontein Dynamite Factory — about 12 kilometres

There is a seldom-visited part of Mountain View that remains idyllic – full of jacarandas with soft shadows and sandstone garages with old, weathered doors. Occasionally, you might notice a feature from a bygone age: a carved wooden spire on the apex of a roof, an outhouse, perhaps, or a sash window. There are converted stables and the sprawl of subdivision and alteration, calmed by a profusion of trees and greenery. Walking here, at the beginning of Hope Road, just off Louis Botha Avenue, is invigorating and spicy. The temperature is lower because of the tree shade, and the trees themselves seem to sponge away some of the suburb's wearying noise. Everything has a drippy, children's hideaway kind of feel, a world of tree houses and secret retreats at the bottom of the garden. It was here, early one Sunday morning in mid-autumn, that I decided to step out and find South Africa.

Hope Road was empty at this early hour. There were no cars rushing down its one-way system along the base of the

Mountain View ridge and the road was mine, giving me a feeling of well-being and mild propriety. The first person I saw was a homeowner on the other side of the street, out with his Weed Eater as he trimmed his square of lawn. He was wearing a white vest and I could see him through a jagged maze of barbed wire as I tumbled past, feeling my daypack (oranges, pens, notebooks) as it settled on my back, the pleasing rise and fall of my legs in my boots. As I walked quickly down Hope, feeling the vitality that comes from purposeful walking, the barbed and razor wire became more noticeable; the seemingly endless categories of domestic defence gave the suburb an embattled, dug-in feel. It was also dirty. I drive my wife mad because my instinct is always to pick up litter but there was so much of it as I approached the foot of Sylvia Pass that it made this task too awkward. There were too many casually discarded beer bottles and cans of Coke, chip wrappers and bottle tops.

Not to be downcast, I looked for beauty and detail. I noticed a carved wooden door, paint fading like a retreating tide, that wouldn't have been out of place in Goa. There were mosaic street numbers and the magical sound of Zen fountains, heard but not seen, bubbling away on the other side of a wall. As I swerved through the kink east of Sylvia Pass, I was greeted by a platoon of planes, their brown leaves crinkly in the breeze. I was now walking more north than east. The aspect changed, the sun suddenly more insistent. As I walked along Ninth Avenue, out of the shade of the planes, I found myself stopping. I turned to face the sun, marvelling at the luxury houses perched on Linksfield Ridge, more impressive than one realises when one drives through the area in a car.

Runners and ramblers began to emerge as I walked down Ninth Street. I noticed a pair of joggers, bright with the latest gear, and a lean man on the opposite side of the street running past me, backwards. I saw a group of three 60-something walkers, chicken legs protruding from baggy shorts, briskly launching themselves into their Sunday-morning ritual. A man came towards me with the Sunday papers under his arm, talking on his mobile, before disappearing slowly into the shadows, looking cold and half asleep. I passed a group of stout, severely pruned trees. Ginkgos or mulberries, they were thick, with trunks like powder kegs. Looking at them in their mute rootedness made me boyishly happy, and I strode out, past the Yiddish kindergarten, down through the avenue of planes and the orange leaves of autumn, heading for the Jewish enclaves of Fairmount, Sydenham and Glenhazel.

Johannesburg's first powered flight took place slightly east of where I was walking, across the grassy cusp of what used to be called Sydenham Hill. Frenchman Albert Kimmerling had shipped out from Southampton on the *Kenilworth Castle* in 1909 as a representative of biplane manufacturer Voisin. His intention was to be the first man to fly in Africa, and he would hopefully pick up orders for the Voisin along the way. Improbably, he and a mechanic decided that East London was the best place in which to make their grab for immortality and Africa's first recorded flight duly took place at the Nahoon Racetrack just after Christmas in 1909. Early the following year, Kimmerling crated his plane up to the Rand. What the *Rand Daily Mail* called 'a special garage' was built on the edge of the Orange Grove flying grounds, and by February he was ready to test the Highveld's thin air in his rickety craft, part pterodactyl, part kite.

The occasion was well organised. Tickets could be bought from the Central News Agency and a flotilla of trams was laid on for spectators to ship down Louis Botha Avenue (then called Johannesburg Road) to Orange Grove. It was an event with a certain shimmer. Flying was the rage in Europe. The year before, John Moisant, the son of an American sugar baron, had dropped in unannounced before 250 000 bewitched spectators at a Paris air show. Here in South Africa, there was less transparent showmanship, although, unlike Paris, refreshments would be served. 'The public will be notified of the conditions as follows,' reported the *Rand Daily Mail* of 1 February 1910. 'A red flag will be flown from the Corner House buildings, the Carlton Hotel and Messrs Cuthbert building at an early hour on Saturday to denote that conditions are good and the flights will take place as advertised between 3–6pm. Should there be no red flag, the flight will not come off.'

February must have been exquisitely frustrating for Kimmerling because it took until the end of the month for the red flag to eventually be raised. On the 26th, watched by a crowd of thousands, Kimmerling shovelled his unstable biplane after what in all likelihood would have been no more than a couple of hundred metres; the craft wouldn't have flown more than three or four metres off the ground. Photographs in Museum Africa in Newtown show the Voisin cheer-fully plunging along an axis almost due south, with Linksfield Ridge in the background.

Had Kimmerling flown in the opposite direction, he would have headed directly for what was to become Moishe's Butch-ery in Raedene, the beginning of the Jewish district. I stopped there for sparkling water and a look around as the cleaning staff were mopping the floor while white-coated butchers (Moishe himself, perhaps?) stood around importantly in white wellies. I remembered an old-fashioned Italian barber in the complex and, nearby, the terminus for the Sydenham bus. The buses in those days were slow, sooty and eternally long-suffering. You paid for your ticket either at the driver's cab or when the conductor came round. He wore two gunfighter's straps that diagonally crossed his chest, upon which hung a sort of primitive cash register on one hip, and on the other a little apparatus with a handle for dispensing tickets. The mobile cash register, consisting of upright cylinders stacked side by side that dispensed change, had its merits but the ticket dispenser was by far the funkier affair. It was solidly silver and had dials and wheels out of which emerged rect-angular little stubs in pastel greens and yellows. At some point in your journey you would wedge your stubs into the back of the seat in front of you, where it would take its place alongside the Neanderthal graffiti, the lewd anatomical draw-ings and the word *'poes'* repeated like a mantra.

From Moishe's, I walked down a gentle hill, the turf spongy beneath my feet, as I approached the Fairmount Shopping Centre. I fell in with a Zimbabwean vendor in an orange

T-shirt. He was selling hand towels, *lappies* and dishcloths, and at first was reluctant to give too much away, telling me simply that he was from 'Africa'. He looked a little like one of those clothes horses you see in tiny European flats, with towels hanging from every portion of his raised arms. I explained my mission and we walked a while before he peeled off to buy something at the Shell garage. I later saw him peddling his wares at the shopping centre roughly opposite the Jewish old aged home. By then his face had assumed the careful neutrality that seems, in part, a defence against the worst, in part, the expectation of that worst. Further down the pavement, on another patch, was another vendor. He was sitting in a canvas camp chair selling Manchester United beach towels, among others, talking football conspiratorially to a mate who was complaining about the poaching of players in club football. They talked in neither a whisper nor the tone of a normal speaking voice, so what they were saying seemed vaguely Byzantine, full of intrigues I couldn't share.

Before reaching the shopping centre, with its kosher deli and outside eating area, the hardware store and Spar supermarket, I stumbled upon the Jabula Recreation Centre. When my sister, Laura, and I were growing up in nearby Lyndhurst, my mother used to bundle us into the car and take us there on a weekly basis. My tastes were non-literary: Asterix and Obelix, Tintin, Lucky Luke and his savvy talking horse, Jolly Jumper. (There is surely a fine book or thesis to be written on Jolly Jumper and Tintin's soliloquising dog, Snowy, who both sidle up to the reader by gently undermining the hero but are fiercely loyal to him at the same time.) I used to read sports books and devour a series published, I think, by Mc-Donalds on countries of the world like Greece or Chile or Turkey. The books followed a pattern, with items on history, exports, religion and landscape. The section I liked most, though, was the story of a day in the life of an average Turkish family: when they would get up, how long the school day lasted, how much homework was mandatory before they could watch television. I loved finding out what the evening meal consisted of, and what they ate and drank, what they dressed in and what they looked like. I used to pore over these books for hours, lost in silent reverie, trying to imagine what it would be like to live in Marmaris or Santiago or Thessaloniki, and if my name was Orhan or Jaime or Costas.

Thinking back on it, the library became almost sacred for me as a child, a place of quiet abandon. When you borrowed books, you handed over your library cards, bright little envelopes of reinforced cardboard. They were slightly rough to touch and fitted neatly into the palm of your hand or the pocket of a school blazer. Mine, I seem to remember, were a bright buttery yellow. Once you had parted with your cards, the books themselves were stamped with a franking punch, jumping through its work with springy zest. The librarian pounded the books' return date onto the thin paper folio gummed to the front of the book, and popular books were crisscrossed with these brief reminders of the return date, sometimes separate, sometimes overlapping. Depending on the colour of ink used, the trails were either mauve or deep purple, charcoal or black, and you could trace them backwards, burrowing into the book itself to find out how old it was. These prints were an index of ancestry. You could distinguish the popular books from the neglected ones, the inspirational from the dull. Such was the anonymous murmur of the critics of suburbia.

The librarians who presided over this calm island wore blue cotton housecoats. There were often triangular pots of milky glue on their desks and sometimes flowers in a vase. I imagine this forgotten world now with infinitely sad longing, indescribable melancholy. I can hear the withdrawal of a thin drawer of stacked catalogue cards and the return of that drawer into the wooden cabinet with crisp finality, a sound almost plush. On summer's days there were invariably fans going about their rhythmical business, looking left then right, like pedestrians crossing the road. They would hum good-naturedly through the silence, a background wash to the franking and stamping and the graceful slide of books back onto the shelf.

* * *

Next door to the Jabula Library was the Community Hall – home, among other things, to Round Table 121, of which my dad had a stint as chairman. Round Table provided the opportunity for fundraising, sometimes with a serious theme – such as their 'evening of ecology' at the German School, guest speaker Ian Player. But sometimes the men simply dressed up as women, wearing massively outsized bras and high heels as they sang songs from a melodrama or bumbled happily through Gilbert and Sullivan's *The Pirates of*

Penzance. I remember black-and-white photographs from the era – or I think I do. The men are wearing jeans with belt buckles the size of Texas, checked shirts and scarves wound rakishly round their necks. My father is in his element, the glint of unchecked madness in his eye.

It was the late 1970s, so a time of fondue sets and dinner parties, of red candlesticks wedged into green Grünberger Stein bottles. My parents were both bohemian and fiercely conventional, so they read Edward de Bono *and* Dick Francis, listened to Jacques Brel *and* Erroll Garner. Looking back on it, I think colleagues and neighbours might have looked at us slightly askance, with a mixture of envy and mild derision. Our dogs, after all, were called Smuts and Brünnhilde. Smuts, the good-natured German shepherd, so called because he had a big patch of white on his breast and this reminded Dad of Jan Smuts's goatee. Brünnhilde was the princess of German mythology from Wagner's opera piece the *Ride of the Valkyries*. Ours had a docked tail and was probably a combination of Alsatian and boxer – we were never quite sure. I somehow doubt that there were many other dogs in the suburb called Smuts and Brünnhilde.

We owned a green Peugeot station wagon and for holidays we perched our igloo tent on a hill overlooking the Hole in the Wall in the Transkei. Dad bartered for lobster with the locals while my mother cooked pork bangers for my sister and me, fried on our portable gas stove, together with a vile instant concoction called Smash, because we didn't fancy the idea of eating lobster. Despite sibling rivalries and patches of marital angst, being pernickety about money, we were, I think, as Tolstoy described, a happy family much the same as all the other happy families in the world.

Behind the community centre and library was a play area. Its main attraction was a jungle gym in the shape of an aeroplane. This was no thrown-together afterthought. It must have been four or five metres long, with wings and a tail fin, and three wooden seats in the nose for the 'pilots'. I'd noticed the aeroplane from the road, and, amazed it was still standing after all these years, edged my way across a damp decline before reaching it. Miraculously, one of its wooden seats was still there and it was, as far as I could see, entirely intact, too cumbersome and well made for the scrap-metal dealers to have cut it up or prised it from the ground. As a boy I spent many enjoyable afternoons in and on the aeroplane, fighting for the pilot seat and taking off through the marshy ground and looping above the surrounding suburbs in my trustworthy old Dakota before landing perfectly, taxiing to a stop exactly where we had started.

I so loved aeroplanes as a child that I made my own back at home in Lyndhurst, building them out of bricks and wooden offcuts I scrounged from the outhouse, launching them into the air through the power of fantasy alone. Laura and I were self-sufficient children. We were constantly playing make-believe games, and making and drawing things. I often played cricket matches against the whitewashed wall of the garage, commentating my way through Test matches between England and Australia, New Zealand and the West Indies. There was no chance of seeing any of these teams live, so I brought them onto our own patch of kikuyu with the clouds of jasmine at deep extra cover and the wooden fence of creosoted planks off to one side. As much as anything else, I was thrilled by the cricketers' names, sensing that they said something about where they came from. Frank Hayes, from Lancashire, was an Englishman; Bev Congdon was the hardbitten New Zealander; Eknath ('what kind of name was that?') Solkar was a fine fielder for India and glamorous beyond compare.

Looking back, there must have been some unrecognised complications. I remember, for example, following the exploits of Maurice Foster, a Jamaican middle-order batsman and occasional off-spinner. Foster boomeranged in and out of the West Indian Test side of the early 70s, always in the frame, never quite cementing a long-term place. With a surname like that, he seemed familiar, yet he couldn't have been completely familiar because he was clearly black. This was a plus in my eyes, although it also suggested that life was possibly more fraught than I cared to think about. Maybe black people came from certain parts of the world and not others, playing cricket for the places from which they came. This was plausible enough, although it had self-evident limitations, because I rubbed shoulders with black people every day of my life and they didn't seem to play much cricket. Instead, they were servants, or men apologetically in search of piecework. I saw them walking down the street, steering clear of the dogs, who shared a sharp communal dislike of black pedestrians. At 10 years of age, I didn't make any connections. In the apartheid of my young mind, these were all separate developments. This was simply how it was.

And none of this could get in the way of the Wednesday

afternoons I looked forward to, when my weekly magazines got delivered to the local newsagent. I remember seeing a team photograph in one of them of the 1973 West Indian tourists to England, with Foster playing his customary peripheral role. They were all wearing maroon blazers, and, as a young fan, I was stunned at how snappy they looked, how they shone. Looking back, it was colour that did it for me: the green of a Springbok jersey, the thick red vertical stripe down the front of Ajax Amsterdam's shirt, the maroon of a West Indian blazer and cap. In political – even literal – terms, we lived in a black-and-white world, yet my eyes and mind were sensitive to explosions of everyday colour.

After touching the metal wings and admiring the fact that the several colours of paint hadn't faded completely from the fuselage, I walked onwards. There was a seen-better-times bowling club on the other side of the Jabula parking lot, with that overgrown, boarded-up feel of holiday houses in winter. Everywhere in this part of Sandringham at this time of a Sunday morning I was pricked by a sadness borne of neglect. There was too much that was once full of life; there was too much that was empty or abandoned, too many relics and ghosts. The bowls club would once have been a happy place, full of the civilised lyrics of the greens, the buttery-slick woods, the jack rolled into place underneath the crêpe sole of a white bowls shoe, the jolly mayhem of the bar. Now weeds were marching across the once pristine verges. The Highveld sun was cracking the paint, time obstinately levering open the doors, the suburb's music sombre and receding.

After the kosher deli and the Zimbabwean vendor, I walked down a gentle slope towards Sandringham High School, heading east through the obscure little suburbs of Glensan, Glenkay and Fairvale. Sandringham itself, on the opposite side of the road, was built to accommodate returning servicemen after World War II, and the names around me seemed to pay homage to imperial Great Britain and the Crown. There were streets called Victoria Road and, although I didn't see them, consulting the map afterwards, I noticed Elizabeth and Wellington avenues. This neck of suburbia had clearly escaped the rage for renaming, although an official with too much time on his hands will shortly be inspired to call Sandringham Julius Nyerere Township and the R25 as it heads towards Edenvale Hospital, Ujamaa Way. Then again, who could fail to see the latent potential in a suburb called Fairvale? Simply add a 'y' and in 'Fairyvale' you'd have one of the smallest and Peter Pan-like of all Johannesburg's suburbs.

Despite its slight twilight-zone feel, this was good walking country. The verges were wide and largely clean, with townhouse complexes and demure blocks of 70s' flats tucked away from the road, looking tantalising behind their curtains of subtropical growth. The traffic was orderly and, filled with a sense of happy well-being, I crossed the road and swung down to the school, noticing the fence by one of its tennis courts had collapsed like a sleeping child. I crossed the intersection of the R25 and Northfield Avenue, tramping on towards Modderfontein. Over to my right, unseen from view, was the Rietfontein Infectious Diseases Hospital, or the Rietfontein Lazaretto, as it was originally known. Built to deal with those who had contracted bubonic plague, smallpox and tuberculosis, it was situated on what were then the city limits. The hospital staff nursed Chinese labourers, Hindus from the so-called 'Coolie Location', and Irish and Polish labourers back to health, doing so under the benevolent gaze of its first superintendent, Dr John 'Max' Mehliss. Nowadays there is a retirement village alongside, and despite protests from amateur historians and heritage officials, it looks as if the entire area, which contains five graveyards of various denominations (the Jewish and leper cemeteries have never been found), will be bulldozed to make room for residential developments.

Mehliss, who cared for the ill from the hospital's inception in 1895 until his death, 32 years later, was an unusually dedicated, gentle man. His formal education was patchy, being limited to a few years at high school in King William's Town, but he managed to impress the authorities at the universities of Munich and Gutenberg (in Mainz) sufficiently for him to be allowed to study further. He was such a precocious student that he once caught the eye of Otto von Bismarck, who commented crisply that he had some cheek to arrive from the colonies and beat the empire's best students in their medical examinations. Although Mehliss discriminated against no one, never turning the sick away on the basis of race or creed, his was not a name that slipped easily off the tongue – a cause, perhaps, for dissatisfaction. 'Mehliss' was corrupted by his patients to 'mealies' or 'Dr Mealies', and the Lazaretto became known as the 'Mealies Hospital'.

* * *

I had decided to walk from Mountain View and Orange Grove to Modderfontein because both suburbs were once home to a sizeable chunk of Johannesburg's Italian community. Some of the first members of that community had been recruited to Modderfontein from the hill town of Avigliana, in north-west Italy, a day or two's brisk walk due west of Turin. Avigliana was the site of one of Alfred Nobel's several European dynamite factories. When Paul Kruger controversially snatched the Transvaal dynamite concession out of private hands, building a new factory on the farms Modderfontein and Klipfontein, he realised that unless he moved quickly, he'd have a staffing crisis on his hands. Today you can still see enlarged photographs of the much sought-after Italians' visas in the Modderfontein Museum. Signed by Italy's King Umberto and granted under the authority of the mayor of Avigliana, they authorise the long trip to the Transvaal 'for reasons of work'. One is for Andrea Molinero, an Avigliana tradesman; he was short, according to the museum item, getting on (33) and, given that he was prepared to undertake the long voyage to Africa from Genoa or Marseilles, probably desperate for work.

Not only were the Italians experienced in working with dynamite, they also came cheap. Unlike the Germans (some of them from Schlebusch, near Cologne) and Austrians (from Nové Zámky), who weren't prepared to work for less than 20 pounds a month, the Italians would work for between 10 and 12. Their process operators, artisans and *cartuccere*, or 'cartridge girls', numbered about 200 when they started coming to South Africa, and they made up by far the largest portion of the European labour contingent when the factory first opened in 1896. At the beginning, along with a substantial number of recruits from the Eerste Fabrieken near Leeufontein, east of Pretoria, they lived in tents on the factory grounds. By and by, their quarters were upgraded to form the 'Italian Village', with structures of permanence as well as pigsties and chicken runs. They made it their home as best they could, sampling local commodities. (Archaeological digs into the tips close to their compound, for instance, have found shards of glass from bottles containing 'Dr Williams' pink pills for pale people'.) As well as spending their hard-earned pounds on this 'multi-purpose panacea', they owned a communal gramophone. On Sundays they used to have picnics on the banks of Dam No. 3, Verdi's operas mingling with the breeze. Photos in the museum show them in front of a large, steep-sided white tent. The men are wearing sandals and collarless shirts, and look casually sophisticated. The women's hair is scraped back and they're wearing white, high-necked dresses. They are healthy, their skin sun-tanned, and they gaze at the camera without demurral. Given their experience and sustaining sense of community, they might even consider themselves the factory's first labour aristocracy.

There was a second, more quixotic, reason for starting my walk where I did. Like many Johannesburgers, I had long been intrigued by the whereabouts of the orange grove in Orange Grove. I'd imagined the grove was on high ground, perhaps on Sydenham Hill, where Kimmerling had bounced his Voisin for Johannesburg's first recorded flight. In my mind's eye, I imagined row upon row of orange trees with glossy leaves, the oranges luminous with sunshine, bright like Christmas-tree decorations. Prim with order, they marched into the distance, neatly Californian. All that remained – or so went the fantasy – was the odd lucky tree in a suburban back yard, sulkily rationing its riches.

After doing some research, I discovered that the grove, such as it was, grew alongside or close to a natural watercourse that still bubbles on the Houghton side of Louis Botha's death bend, possibly on one of the oldest farms in the vicinity, called Lemoen Plaas. This stream provided the water for a covered swimming pool close to where the BP garage was until recently, although it is difficult to pinpoint exactly the swimming pool's location. This is because old photographs of the area are slightly ambiguous. Was the resort's pool close to the slip road just off Louis Botha, in the vicinity of where the La Rustica restaurant used to be? Or was it slightly further down the road, at the junction of Osborne Road and Louis Botha? It is almost impossible to say exactly, because the area on the southern side of Louis Botha has been built upon, the sense of scale is iffy and no natural landmarks remain because everything has been drowned in brick and concrete. There's a union headquarters, followed by an old block of flats set back from the road and, after that, a corporate park the entrance to which is exactly opposite Hope Road's south-western end. The situation was compounded by the fact that, strictly speaking, the orange grove probably wasn't in Orange Grove at all. To be officious, it was in what subsequently came to be known as Mountain View.

Wherever the resort's home and the exact location of the

grove were, it was a place to which the leisured classes of early Johannesburg were readily attracted. Old sepia-washed postcards show lawns dotted with thatched gazebos and pathways on which to stroll. The resort or guest farm was a place to which you could come to sip afternoon tea and take in the soothing waters of the Sand Spruit. At the height of the resort's popularity, balloon rides were offered, underscoring the area's early fascination with flight. As for the orange trees, they might have been the subject of the early workings of the Joburg publicity machine, perhaps the fantasy of a wildly optimistic town planner. There was unlikely to have ever been a grove. It was probably more like a group of orange and other fruit trees mixed with the willows and tall wattles of the spa, although a clue is to be found in the name of the old farm itself. Does Lemoen Plaas not suggest the presence of trees? A lovely article by Brett McDougal published by the Heritage Portal in February 2016 alerts us to the easy connection between Lemoen Plaas and Orange Grove. He also mentions that the suburb had early problems with name and identity. It was called Alexandra, Alexandria Estate and even Cellieria, before finally settling down to long domestic bliss as Orange Grove.

* * *

After passing the hidden remains of the Rietfontein Lazaretto, I found myself skipping down a well-used path that leads to the Jukskei River as it passes beneath the R25. The path here had been softly excavated by many anonymous feet and was, at times, root-crossed and magical in a mossy, Hobbit-like way, deep-sided with time and history. There were dusty old cypresses tucked just inside the fence of the retirement village I was passing, and I was sure the path was broken by the roots of those trees, obdurately seeking out warmth and water and the nutrients of the soil.

The walk here had an airy, big-sky feel. The National Health Laboratory Service offices were over to my left, and the views were good and open as I banged down towards what was probably the walk's lowest point, before crossing the river and negotiating my way over a concrete culvert. After that it was head-down stuff. The incline past the Edenvale Hospital didn't offer a challenging gradient but the heat was gathering. I'd been walking quickly and there was now a teeth-gritting, feel-it-in-my-legs dimension to the walk. I sensed the sweat pooling in the small of my back as I nudged up the hill, crossing the road as I watched a group of scrap-metal collectors ferrying their load in the same general direction. There were two or three of them, and they seemed to have difficulty steering their trolley with any degree of even short-term control. This meant they needed frequent stops to realign the trolley wheels and gather breath. It was hot and their load heavy as they inched like Catholic penitents slowly up the hill.

Having passed the entrance to the Edenvale Hospital, the R25 curled left to cross the highway down below, before heading past the turn-offs to the new industrial park (left) and the Greenfields Shopping Centre (right). I crossed over to the shade of some pine trees, seeking the softness of the needle-strewn ground. Heading on, it was all concrete along the

overpass, cars now brushing past me as they surged for Edenvale, just down the road, Kempton further afield and sometimes the Modderfontein turn-off.

I grew up in Lyndhurst, vaguely behind me, first in a block
of flats called Hessenford and then in a comfortable but very
ordinary tin-roofed house at 55 Lyndhurst Road. From certain vantage points in the suburb you could look east and
see the area through which I was now walking. It was all
farmland then, dominated by a thick clot of blue gums and
evergreens that a farmer seemed happy to preserve. The
image is fixed in my mind because beyond that, unseen, lay
Modderfontein Dynamite Factory, where my father spent
many adventurous years being what in those days was called
a personnel manager. Sooner or later, either because of a veld
fire or lightning strike, and sometimes through malfunction
or human error, we would hear the deep reverberations of a
faraway explosion. It was Dad's responsibility to get onto
the plant immediately – at one time Modderfontein was
referred to as a national key point – to find out what had happened and, if necessary, notify next of kin if lives had been
lost. In the excitement and fear we experienced as children
after an explosion, we would scan the sky for telltale signs,
sometimes seeing a thin vine of smoke creeping upwards
before it disappeared.

There was little left of the copse of trees now, although
stragglers and an island of well-established pines remained as
the R25 split into separate eastbound and westbound lanes.
The walking during this period of the route was unpleasant
and tricky, a constant effort of negotiation. It was impossible

to walk in a straight line, so I had to tack across islands and skirt sets of lights, no provision being made for pedestrians. Cars strained like dogs on a leash as they awaited the green light, gunning down the hill beside me, and I felt simultaneously exposed and invisible, feeling a sort of shadow emotion of what it must be like for so many of the walking urban poor. I remember during this portion of the walk picking my way across a verge and noticing the confetti of discarded takeaway packets, cheap booze bottles and plastic under some young white maples. The homeless and impromptu car washers, the beggars and hands-free-kit salesmen had camped here for the night, hunkering down when their provisions ran out, trying to forget the gathering cold as it gnawed at their bones.

Eventually, the walking began to take on a less claustrophobic, less insistently urban feel. I nosed down the Modderfontein slip road while the R25 spun away down the hill, off to the east and the nondescript formlessness of Edenvale's townhouse sprawl, each house apparently different, all actually the same. The Modderfontein shops weren't far away and after a period walking on gravel alongside the road, the path became paved and neatly finished. Restored bangers trundled past me on their Sunday-morning vintage-car outing, buffed and proud, and a sense of fun and frivolity washed over me. Children were having a birthday party in the canopy of pine trees on my right and it seemed more relaxed here, more obviously Sunday morning-ish, now that I had wriggled free of the concrete and the mania. I picked up a pine cone to take home and threaded past a newly refurbished

Shell garage, two men sitting sipping coffee in a sunlight-flooded window. I found an old café, tended by a Bangladeshi watching a poorly tuned television, the picture speckled with snowflakes. I bought an ice cream and two square banana-flavoured toffees, and took them down to the grass. I sat down beside the first of Modderfontein's dams. My first walk over, I texted my wife to come and collect me, and started jotting down my impressions and drawing diagrams with wry captions. It was a Sunday morning. The sun was shining and folk were walking their dogs on the lawn at the edge of the dam, the dogs' tails wagging, their noses wet with the simple blessing of being alive.

* * *

One cold Saturday morning a couple of weeks later, I drove back to Modderfontein to nail down the final plank of the story. I was met by security at the entrance to the dynamite plant and escorted inside before leaving my car and being chaperoned to the factory cemetery. The graveyard was large and dusty, neither perfectly tended nor completely ignored. There were shrivelling flowers on some of the graves, and although the grass and weeds hadn't taken over completely, everywhere time was going about its earnest work, nudging the crosses in the faraway black section of the cemetery over the perpendicular, nibbling away at the headstones and the masonry. There were glum cypresses inside the wrought-iron gate, some jacarandas with yellow-green winter leaves and a bottlebrush or two. The colours were muted. We instinctively whispered, gesture and word being squared-off to the minimum. You could feel the early-morning chill muzzle about your legs, and the cloying sadness of the place was impossible to shake.

I was here because in April 1898, approximately two years after arriving from Avigliana, a group of 15 *cartuccere* lost their lives in an explosion. Their precautions, like wearing pinafores and working in bare feet, had been of no use, for they were obliterated. So poor were the families from which they came, and so reluctant the factory authorities to contribute anything to their gravestones or memorial, that only three of the 15 are commemorated in the cemetery. Two are sisters – Margarithe and Anna Tonda; the third a young woman called Margarithe Gugno, who lies next to the sisters in numbered grave 161. The granite memorial erected to commemorate them is dominating but simple, with the words '*Qui riposino* – killed in an explosion' stencilled down one side. As I wandered down the pathways, looking half-heartedly for the other graves, it became clear that these early artisans faced daily danger of a kind unheard of today. I noticed two gravestones for Alfred Pleitz, who died on Christmas Day 1896; Bernard Schmedding and Theodore Volkmann both died two years later. Maria Columbino, buried nearby, lost her life in 1907. Everywhere were the dead and their losing battle with oblivion – one that is likely to be escalated in the near future because much of the land has been sold to a consortium of Chinese property developers with big plans for residential compounds and even a university.

My guide, Peet Hattingh, from plant security, kindly pointed out several things that I had missed. The ornate wrought-iron fence wrapped around the Tonda memorial came from HCE Eggers and Co., Hamburg. It, the memorial stones, and the cost of transportation, must have been significant. He pointed out the tiny Italian flags on the Italians' graves and told me how the plant had shrunk since his arrival way back when. As he drove me back to my car in one of the plant security's bakkies, I could see the neurotic order in which the factory and surrounds were still preserved. Now it looked more like a beautifully maintained industrial museum than a functioning plant. Once it had been thriving. Goods wagons rolled into the heart of the factory to take the gelignite directly to the Rand mines.

Such was the site's importance that, until 1948, the country's weather forecasts came from Modderfontein. Padding round the museum one weekday morning I'd seen photographs of the weather station, a strange raised structure that looked like a Tyrolean cabin, all pitched roof and ornate exterior woodwork. Looking at the photo inspired me to imagine the weatherman, surrounded by his barometers and wind vanes. He was standing on his balcony, looking south at the cumulus clouds, stacked like purple grapes in the sky, wondering when the storm would arrive and, if it did, where lightning would strike.

2
ONE 'MENEER' OF A WALK

Salem, south-west of Grahamstown, to
Southwell — about 24 kilometres

A couple of days before my walk in 'frontier country', I met a pilgrim, my first. For technical reasons, our flight to Port Elizabeth was delayed and the pilgrim and I had found ourselves close by, stranded back in the departure lounge, wondering if we could grab a quick coffee before being called to reboard. Although I have forgotten his name, there was something about him I liked. He seemed uninhibited in a trustworthy, vaguely shambolic kind of way, a man without narcissism or artifice. We got chatting and he mentioned that he had jetted in overnight from Tel Aviv (I noticed a wodge of Israeli postcards jutting out of his daypack) after spending three weeks in Jerusalem visiting churches, meeting clergy and proselytising.

About seven or eight years ago he had nearly died, he told me with careless intimacy. Several specialists had advised that the tumours (one behind the eye, one buried deep in his brain) were too invasive and therefore inoperable, and he had shrivelled up at the news, frightened and depressed. There was a hereditary predisposition in his family, he said, to high blood pressure and blockages, and there was nothing to be done. He couldn't afford to go overseas for treatment, and the local specialists – he named them – were rude and jocularly dismissive. He knew he was going to die.

One night, he heard voices, and jerked out of bed. The voice was close and not unfamiliar, very real to him in an almost physical, reach-out-and-touch kind of way. It bade him to convert and open his heart to the Lord, which he did. Miraculously, his health improved, and after having been given only months to live, he had now been healthy for years. He had gone to Israel to share his story but found it a challenge because, for some reason I can't now remember, he had difficulty walking. There was something wrong with his foot, and he found the Jerusalem taxi drivers money-grabbing and ill-mannered. He compared himself to John the Baptist, one of the Bible's famous walkers, and, like him, he was now a disciple. Although he bubbled with a busy fervour that was not mine, he seemed happy, and somehow unburdened and unashamed. What he said was less important than how he said it. He was zealous, yes, but also radiantly calmed. He wasn't a sophisticated man but, without being able to exactly articulate why, I felt pleased to have met him. We were called to board through a gate on the level above us and although I looked for him, he was nowhere to be found. I didn't see him on the flight and, although I looked again, he wasn't at the luggage carousel either. I sometimes wonder if I met him at all.

* * *

A couple of days later, on a mild Saturday morning, three of us started our walk from the hamlet of Salem, which is nothing more, really, than a Methodist church and a frost-crusted cricket pitch with a pink gush of bougainvillea between the two. My two companions were Craig Paterson and Jako Bezuidenhout, postgraduate students in the History department at Rhodes University. I'd met Craig in the course of researching a story on the history of indigenous horse racing in the Eastern Cape a couple of months previously, and on our long drives through the former Transkei we'd discussed the possibility of a walk.

The group had swelled because Craig felt Jako would be up for such an adventure and for weeks we'd haggled about a route. Craig wanted to walk the old wagon road from the hinterland to the coast, an idea I liked, but I was also keen on somehow walking past Theopolis, the now ruined site of a former frontier mission station. The problem with the two ideas, hopelessly romantic as they were, was that both the wagon route and Theopolis were on private land. Eastern Cape farmers are by and large a beleaguered lot, caught between the pincers of government land reform on the one hand and the vagaries of the market on the other. They weren't going to respond well to slacker writers and leftie academics tramping over their land in search of gravestones and artefacts. Land restitution is a hot political potato in the Eastern Cape and the commonage around Salem had just been returned to the indigenous local community – a landmark case in the high court, with much learned comment on both sides. We weren't going to tempt fate and so, armed with nothing more sinister than our curiosity and a half-jack of splendidly vile Night's Watch whisky, we stuttered down to Salem in

Craig's put-upon Golf. The idea was to walk to Bathurst if we could, and if that proved too arduous (it was a walk of nearly 50 kilometres) we would bail at Southwell – approximately halfway. Rain was forecast for midnight on the Saturday and although Jako knew of a local farmer who would allow us to pitch our tent in the grounds of the Southwell Club, secretly we were all hoping that we might somehow find a bed.

Maybe Jako knew something about the local farmers that we didn't, because he chose to walk in infantry browns, including the hat. His only concession to civilian attire was a white Reebok T-shirt and a pair of takkies, but he immediately spoiled this slight softening of his image as an *egte* right-winger by bringing a loaf of sliced government white. This he shoved into one of the pockets of his infantryman's jacket and every so often he would nibble furtively from his rations. 'If only my liberal Joburg friends could see me now,' I joked, looking at Jako with mock distaste. We all laughed before trundling up the hill, noting the weight of our packs and adjusting our bodies to accommodate them, feeling the comfort of our feet in our boots and shoes, the simple joy of movement and being gloriously alive.

We made an interesting sight. Our packs were different, our clothing mismatched. I was in shorts, Craig was in jeans, Jako was in browns; I had a cap, Craig had nothing and Jako had his infantryman's cap with clips on the side so you could fold up the brim. Best of all, we were lugging a five-litre bottle of water. We couldn't attach this to any of the packs, so we took turns to carry it along. We looked ill-prepared, with grids fastened to pack straps at the last minute and the happy-go-lucky feel of okies on the march. Still, the weather was good and the day bright. The predicted rain seemed a long, long way away, as we trudged beside the single-lane tar road to Port Alfred for nine kilometres, passing the occasional grove of eucalyptus and stepping aside to let the four-by-fours and overloaded bakkies roar past.

We were chirpy in the beginning, walking well and making good time, our five-litre keg of water swinging jauntily from its plastic handle or being passed from hand to hand. After a couple of kilometres we noticed a troop of vervet monkeys, one of them sitting nonchalantly in the middle of the road. The troop were foraging in an old mielie field, the stalks dry and the once green leaves of the corn rustling thinly in the wind. The field was on our right as we walked but the monkeys had swarmed in from our left. If you looked carefully you could see the remnants of their pillage, the hard, golden-red kernels of corn, a discarded cob here and there. In the scrub separating the road and the fields there were corn leaves caught on the thorns, the vervets' calling cards being nibbled by the wind.

Land restitution claims in this part of the world seemed to have resulted in an awkward truce. Those who lost land were twitchy and embittered (the Salem commonage included the church and cricket pitch, which were now theoretically in the claimants' hands), while those who had benefited believed a historical injustice had been put to right. The case was interesting because the community had been offered the choice of either financial compensation or the land itself and had plumped for the latter, with a representative being quoted in the Grahamstown press saying they were keen on farming. Evidence on the ground, as it were, was meagre. There were a couple of large, green water tanks on the hills and a sense of low-scale irrigation. White farmers we spoke to later were dubious of such initiatives. They felt an element of the 'show trial' result in the high court's decision but, more important-ly, they told us that insufficient distinction was made between subsistence and large-scale commercial farming. The recently returned land was unlikely to produce crops with big enough yields to make sense in commercial terms. While this seemed fair enough, I wondered about the symbolic value of the return. How, emotionally, must the claimants have felt after having been deprived for so long? I imagined that, whatever they did with the land, there would have been a sense of closure, a sense of satisfaction at justice finally having been done.

Then again, this might be so much facile liberalism, maybe something of what John Berger has called 'infantile proletari-anism'. The farmers here were henpecked by legislation and frightened of the future. They graded the roads themselves and faced the ever-present prospect of cattle rustling. They were linked not only by association – the same family names invariably crop up: Amm, Shaw, Bradfield, Stirk, Ford, Kee-ton – and the fact that they were wizards of technology, but also by history and rootedness. They knew the story of the land and who came from where. They knew of the forts and redoubts, the drifts and the secret river meanders. They also found themselves charmed by my companions. 'The settlers came from industrial cities, they knew nothing about farming,' Jako told us. 'The few Afrikaans farmers on the land found themselves in a quandary because they knew potatoes weren't planted on top of the soil. Should they be neighbourly and point out the error of the *Engelsman*'s ways, or should they bide their time and, then, when the farms went bust, buy them up at rock-bottom prices?'

After about two hours' walking, we reached the gravel-road turn-off. We stopped, drank water, and munched on chocolate and meat sticks. The day was wonderful – warm without being hot, with the tug of a gentle breeze. We eased off our packs and I took off my sweater, suddenly feeling the chill of the pooled sweat in the small of my back. We joked and cavorted, all soberly aware of the road ahead, trying to delay our restart for as long as we could.

Gathering up, it wasn't long before we reached the turn-off for the Assegai River. The views were bigger and better, the countryside mixed scrub and farmland. We passed family homesteads, the men sitting outside on upturned beer crates, shooting the breeze, the children following us briefly, much amused comment and shaking of heads about the self-evident foolhardiness of walking to Southwell. The deeper we seeped into the countryside, the more removed from Grahamstown and Salem we felt, and so we plunged into the quiet, only our footfalls and the scuffing of our boots on the gravel road to keep us company. At one point we were passed by a mountain-biker, humourlessly intent on getting to his destination. The episode – almost silent, quickly over – had a surreal, Alice in Wonderland-ish feel to it and we laughed as he bounced away, his legs frantically pedalling in that comical, slightly exaggerated way of mountain-bikers. After a long downhill, our legs beginning now to get really tired, we reached the causeway of the Kariega River for lunch, probably the lowest point of our march. Craig and Jako took off their takkies and boots to bathe their feet. We drank Game and wolfed cheese-and-salami sandwiches, and basked in the quiet, gazing tiredly at the creep of winter water as it lazed towards the sea, congratulating ourselves on time well made.

The route immediately after lunch was punishing – a long series of misleadingly torturous climbs off the valley floor. This was dairy-farming country and there were parcels of lush pastureland all around, bright green in the softening afternoon sun. The wind came up and our pace slowed as we slogged back to higher ground. The southern horizon was building up with cloud and my thoughts began to turn to where we might spend the night. We'd manage in a tent, even in rain, although it would be cramped. But it wouldn't be my first choice, and I wondered if perhaps we might find ourselves on the clubhouse floor, using dusty cushions as makeshift mattresses, surrounded by faded posters and team photos, and long-outdated calendars from the Port Alfred butchery.

We must have walked around 15 kilometres at this point, perhaps a little more. We were stopping more frequently but such were our relations with each other – I knew Craig reasonably well, Jako not at all – that the dictates of machismo forbade any admission of fatigue. So we soldiered on, plodding gently upwards, only to find that we had reached a false rise, which meant that we had to do it all over again. Talk here centred on the South African historians they admired. There was slight grouchiness about Charles van Onselen, although this was trumped by grudging admiration, and we fell into discussion about Noel Mostert's *Frontiers*, the epic story of ragged conflict between the settlers and the Xhosa people. 'That's a *meneer* of a book,' said Jako in his droll Eastern Cape way, and we laughed, the mirth taking our minds off our sore feet and the increasingly heavy weight on our backs.

There were nine so-called 'kaffir' or 'frontier' wars fought over land like this between roughly 1780 and 1880, which amounted pretty much to a hundred years of constant war, with periods of watchful truce between. Jako and Craig's sympathies would vacillate between the oppressors and the oppressed, sometimes finding that there weren't clear distinctions between the two. They knew, for example, that the settlers had been forsaken. They often came from big industrial cities (there was a strong Luddite component in the settler community, Craig said) and had little knowledge or experience of farming. Their skills were few, their hearts frightened, their nights dreadful. Contrast this with the Xhosa, who felt invaded and therefore belittled, fearful that this was a beginning of something that wouldn't end. Was there enough land for them all? Would the heathens soon be on their way? Skirmishes and cattle rustling were year-round sports and the mutual incomprehension was stark. The Xhosa didn't understand how men could wear blouses and watch the night sky for portents, while the settlers couldn't comprehend how

43

you could move cattle across land in search of sweeter grazing, not fencing them in pens or corrals. They looked at each other from across the bluffs of rivers like the Kariega and were united in misunderstanding and fear-crazed loathing.

Craig and Jako's ambivalence was deepened, I would hazard, by the fact that the settlers left behind material remains. The imaginative engagement with the past is in some sense tactile, predicated on being able to walk in a church graveyard or run the palm of your hand across a collapsed gravestone. Culturally, they were closer to the settlers – we all were – but they also felt aggrieved on the Xhosa's behalf. Reflexively, they didn't like the idea of dispossession but neither did they like the idea of distant Cape Town elites using the settler farmers as a bulwark against the tribes. It seemed too shamelessly cynical. 'These guys were just fed to the wolves,' Jako said at one point, and I agreed.

But it was also more complicated than straightforward ambivalence. Jako was writing his MA thesis on the forced removal of communities in Kouga, Colchester and Klipfontein to a patch of barren land called Glenmore on the edge of the old Ciskei. In 1979 the apartheid government dubbed these indigent and unemployed people 'redundant', and they were rounded up, herded into trucks and dumped as far away from anyone else as possible, an eyesore as far as white South Africa was concerned. The government attempted to sanitise the move by spinning a yarn that the removed communities would find decent schools and clinics, parks and community halls. Glenmore was to become, in effect, 'a model township'. It became nothing of the sort.

Many years later, the new post-apartheid government eventually offered 'the redundant' compensation amounting to about R130 000 per removed family, just as long as claims were submitted within the stipulated time. With the help of human-rights lawyers, the former Klipfontein residents managed to lodge their claim on time, whereas those originally from Kouga and Colchester failed to meet the deadline. Although the deadline was extended, those from Kouga and Colchester once again failed to meet the cut-off date, while those from Klipfontein were by now receiving their compensation. What you had, therefore, was the creation of a group of 'haves' within the Glenmore community, while those originally from Kouga and Colchester remained 'have-nots', unable to muster enough resources or energy to complete the paperwork.

According to Craig and Jako, all this disappointment and anger were concentrated in one person, an old man from Glenmore who was dubbed a 'serial window breaker' by *Grocott's Mail*, Grahamstown's weekly newspaper. His name was Ben Mafani and every two years or so he would catch a taxi from Glenmore to Grahamstown, a trip of about 50 kilometres one way, and walk to the back of the high court. Once there, he would find a rock and in full sight of passers-by, lob it through one of the court windows. His first experience of one-man protest resulted in arrest and temporary imprisonment, although the case was eventually dropped. Several years later and after letters aplenty to the government and public protector had been ignored, he refined the democratic process by painting the rock he lobbed through the high-court window: white to symbolise freedom, black 'because my people are sitting in a bad place' and red because 'my people are crying blood'. For this act of political audacity, Mafani was re-arrested and released on R300 bail, according to the South African Press Association's parliamentary correspondent, Ben Maclennan, who has heroically followed the Glenmore case since the very beginning. Mafani's trial resulted in the government belatedly taking the case of those dumped at Glenmore seriously and finally brought the issue of compensation into the foreground, although I have been unable to ascertain whether Mafani's was a generalised protest or one specifically on behalf of those who couldn't complete the requisite paperwork.

Later research confirmed that Glenmore was more than simply a twilight zone for the unwanted. Soon after the removals started, they stopped, because it was belatedly realised that without employment opportunities the model township would never take off. For those already relocated, the situation unfolded like a cruel farce. They couldn't return to Colchester or Kouga because they had no homes to which to return. They were hardly likely to experience much of a future in Glenmore either because the social experiment they were once part of had officially been terminated. And so they hung in a kind of absurd suspended animation: unable to go back and incapable of going forward. Much like the original settlers, they were the damned and the forsaken – weightless people in placeless places, eternally trapped in a country-and-western ballad by Kenny Rogers or Merle Haggard.

According to a monograph published by Maclennan for the South African Institute of Race Relations in 1987, the folk trapped in Glenmore found themselves for the most part in poorly made or incomplete houses. The slats that passed for walls were seldom nailed cleanly to their frames and neither were the walls plastered. Often the walls didn't reach the asbestos roof, meaning heat was lost in winter and the houses were draughty all year round. Water piped from the Fish River was impure and gastroenteritis was rife, as were malnutrition, septicaemia and keratomalacia (the clouding of the cornea due to vitamin deficiency). There were very few shops in the area but the few that were there mercilessly jacked up their prices. A bag of mielie-meal, which sold normally for R8.40 at Boesmansrivier, cost R14.60 when bought from the store at Tyefu. Bread usually cost 17 cents a loaf but prices were raised to 20 cents by shopkeepers with stores closer to Glenmore.

The community also discovered that, with the move from the coast, their buying power contracted. Employment opportunities had been by no means abundant where they came from but people understood their environment and knew their neighbours. There were circuits of patronage and networks of support. Scarce though it was, money could be made, which wasn't the case in Glenmore. People stared at their hands and watched their children wither away, believing themselves to be cursed. 'In this place we are all hungry,' Maclennan quotes a herbalist as saying. 'Soon we will have to eat our children like pigs.' As they became hungrier and sicker, they realised that there was ample free supply of one thing they hadn't considered – coffins. A consignment had been trucked up from Grahamstown and housed in the superintendent's office. 'So when a person or child died you just went to the superintendent and took the size of coffin you wanted, free of charge,' Maclennan quoted a resident as saying.

As the afternoon shadows lengthened, so we, too, became trapped and forsaken. All we wanted to do was sit down but we realised that by sitting down we might never be able to get up, so we resisted the temptation and plodded on in that slightly tentative, pain-wracked way of men dying on their feet. It wasn't a very active form of resistance (we were too tired to actively resist anything), more like a grumpy form of limited passive resistance. Given that we were barely able to put one foot in front of the other by this point, very soon our resistance crumbled and, without perhaps even realising it, we were again sitting down. We hadn't discussed sitting down. It was more like sleepwalking, or a kind of zombie seance. Suddenly we were on our bums, happy in the silent knowledge that we weren't walking. But the problem with sitting down wasn't only that we mightn't be able to get up again – it was far more fundamental. It meant that we were getting no closer to our destination. This was our terrible problem, and a *qua* problem; it was something we actively tried not to think about. The problem was therefore compounded because problems can only be solved – what would the correct verb be in the circumstances? – by the *application* of one's mental faculties. As we were sitting down, numbed by tiredness, there was very little that was active at this point about mind, body or spirit. We were, to coin one of Jako's many colourful Eastern Cape phrases, *vrot* with fatigue, particularly the creeping and insidious mental fatigue that comes from not thinking about what we should be applying our collective mind to. We were a bright lot, after all. We had many postgraduate degrees to rub together, and papers, articles, books. We were very, very learned. Yet at this point we couldn't think, couldn't even think about thinking. We were too tired. Our walking had, in fact, crippled us in every sense. Yet we had no alternative but to walk because only by walking could we stop walking, if you see what I mean. It was a predicament of veritably Glenmore-type proportions.

During one of these frequent stops, when we were trying not to think about the consequences of stopping, we happened to sit down beside what we thought was a field of bright-red salad tomatoes. Craig investigated and discovered that what we'd seen were, in fact, dinky little pimentos. We passed a pimento or two round, wondering if this was dinner for the night. We would all sit here, drink the last of our water and quietly collapse, possibly removing our packs, but probably not bothering. Thankfully, one of us had the presence of mind to reach out into the wider world and it was roundabout here that Jako felt the time had come to phone his farmer contact. Craig and I listened to the conversation carefully. The farmer said we were pretty close to the edge of his property. Just a kilometre or two down the road on the left-hand side was a fort he was busy restoring. We didn't have far to go, he said, with the galling brio of drivers underestimating distance because they spend so much time in their cars. He'd meet us there shortly. Of course, we didn't realise then how long it would take us to walk the last stretch, so with what remained of our energy and good humour we lugged our packs onto our backs and headed off. It couldn't have been more than 20 or 25 minutes before we met Colin Stirk, the farmer, and his wife, Lyn, but it seemed like a life-time – a lifetime of pain.

After preliminaries and handshakes, Colin insisted on show-ing us his restored fort or, to give it its official name, the Woodlands Fort. It once had a fig tree creeping through the roof from inside, he told us, and showed us the new timbers and plasterwork, the new shiny roof. Colin was proud of the restoration, and I noticed, despite my tiredness, that his chest seemed to puff out a couple of inches as he narrated the tale, a quickening of his tone and timbre. The fort had been on the property for well over 150 years, he said, and in his family for as long. It was interesting listening to him talk because I sensed he almost felt obliged to restore the fort, without being able to fully understand why. There was no great financial advantage to be gained. He wouldn't house people or attract tourists. It was simply something that need-ed to be done, a primal duty or rite of passage. He needed to make his mark and place himself and his family in the folds of the surrounding land and therefore history. Restoring the fort was a means of nailing it all down.

I encountered much of this impulse in frontier country – the desire to locate and understand. It had the shape and charge, I think now, of something almost metaphysical, a spiritual longing to establish something continuous and intact, a tradition, perhaps, or a story. This urge to write things down, to preserve them and put them in a frame on the wall has always been important for the descendants of the settlers. It was more so now, I would hazard, because they felt besieged. Colin had just lost two of his prize cows, he told us later. The thief had been a trusted and well-liked member of staff, who had expertly cut them up and shuttled them quickly to Umtata. Colin and Lyn had attended the trial in Grahamstown and noticed the former employee couldn't look them in the eye when he was taken down to the holding cells. They were comforted by the fact that they knew who had butchered the cows only because a watchful member of staff had become suspicious, and she had had the courage to tip them off.

In retrospect, I realise that Colin and Lyn didn't quite know what to make of us. They didn't often encounter three dishevelled walkers (one of them in army browns) pounding in from Salem and, although they were curious, they remained watchfully hospitable for an hour or two as they made up their minds. It helped when Colin asked me as we were bouncing along in his bakkie on the road back to the farmhouse if we'd like a bed for the night. I'd long cast false modesty aside and said yes, we would, with unseemly haste. Before long we were each shown comfortable, tastefully appointed bedrooms, with a shower at the end of the corridor. When we next looked, there was a beer in our hands. Colin fired up the braai and we got to know one another. Craig and I silently exchanged glances as Jako started charming Lyn with stories of his brother's challenged years as a teenager. He blew up postboxes and ran an informal plumbing business on the side, redirecting sink outlet pipes when the fever gripped. Once he even forced a neighbour to flee to Cradock because of a threatening note he stuck to his door. I don't know what Craig was thinking, but I was thinking that we'd landed pretty well. We could have been looking for dry wood and grilling wors on a verge outside of the Southwell Club, wondering if, snug in our sleeping bags, we were going to be woken by rain in the middle of the night.

Soon Colin snapped open his laptop and we were looking at Google Earth images of vacant fields outside of Port Alfred. If you looked carefully you could see wagon-track fingers pointing into the interior. Some overlapped, some were separate, yet they were all clear and remarkably consistent, pointing in the general direction of where we were now. The wagons would have been loaded when the Kowie River was still deep and navigable enough to support a small functioning harbour. Lighters used to flutter in from Port Elizabeth or Cape Town, and maybe even Knysna or George, and discharge knots of apprehensive settlers on the quayside. I can only imagine their trepidation, the Bibles and muskets, the bags of flour and seed, perhaps a hoe perched on top of their pile of meagre possessions. The settlers would have squinted into the harsh African sunlight and noticed the sharply defined shadows, the call of the wild in the dense green bush, and wondered what on earth they were doing.

The following morning, just after breakfast and the best sleep in the world, we all met Colin's dad, Lynn. Colin had phoned him the night before, in the first flush of excitement after our arrival, and wanted him to pop round. Colin's old man told him that he couldn't come because, although it was only 8 p.m., he was already in bed. Standing close by, admiring some old photographs as I overheard their conversation, I smiled inwardly. Colin so desperately wanted his excitement to be his old man's, yet there was something hit-and-miss to his strivings, as there so often is in family situations. As a middle-aged man with a mother who had recently died and a father who was beginning to show signs of neediness, I understood the exchange deep in my heart. I understood that the roles of father and son were now inverting. Despite the fact that Colin would have to wait, there was something tender here and universal. It made me like Colin more than I already did.

Sipping coffee around the big kitchen table on Sunday morning, Lynn told us that he was trying to write a book, an autobiography of sorts. It was not going well. He found himself in quicksand, unable to move, but he hoped that our visit to Theopolis later that morning would provide inspiration. First, though, we needed to visit St James's church, swing past Southwell's old school hall and have a look at the old clay tennis courts at the Southwell Club, with their quaint, salt-painted tramlines. The foundation stone at St James was laid in August 1870 and little more than a year later the church was officially opened by a reverend called Stumbles. 'After a cold lunch,' records Doris Stirk in her *Southwell Settlers*, 'the bishops and clergy left for Grahamstown in their buggies and traps, while the remainder, in spite of the rain, partook of a sumptuous tea which was provided by the Southwell ladies, and a sale of fancy articles, which together with the offertory, brought in the sum of £61 to pay off debts accrued on the building.'

We walked around the little church and the graveyard, noticing the thick-set old lemon trees and casually abundant hydrangeas. I pocketed two lemons, comfortingly fat and knobbly, to take home to my wife, and we poked around the graveyard, Craig and Jako poring over collapsed headstones as we tried to picture how things were, looking for a way to access the graveyard as one might open a book. I stood for a quiet minute in the free-standing bell cubicle next to the church, noticing a plaque bearing an inscription to George Ford and his wife, Doris May (née Stirk), erected by their children in 1969. Everywhere in settler country, I noticed, was the same gyre of names looping back through space and time, the circles and ceaseless continuities. They spun back to Southwell, the village in Nottinghamshire from which these settlers came, yet admitted none but their own, the circle closed to other names and deeds and histories. Names associated with 'coloured' people and, to use the historical colonial term, the 'Hottentots' (the Khoikhoi), like Whitbooy Levellot and Ruyter Apollos, appear in records and books from round about this time. As a rule, however, the names of black people do not. As far as they are concerned, there are seldom written records and certainly no church grave-yards. Their dead remain sharply forgotten, bones in the veld, neglect begetting further neglect.

In the graveyard we discovered a headstone commemo-rating the life of one William Gray – '... killed in action near the Karraa by the rebel Hottentots of Theopolis ...' – and, then, less than an hour later, found ourselves on the farm on which Theopolis was situated, currently the property of the generous Howson Long, a wiry man with greying hair and a gunslinger's moustache. We were hoping to find a small group of graves, particularly those belonging to the family of the Reverend George Barker. The reverend and his wife, Sarah Williams, were married in London in 1815 and arrived in South Africa the following year. Their intention had been to serve in Robert Moffat's missionary station in Kuruman, but Sarah's ill-health prevented her from making the journey north. They joined Rev. Ulbricht as members of the London Missionary Society at the Theopolis Mission instead.

By all accounts, Barker was an enterprising and warm-hearted man. He made his own nails in the smithy and whenever he was asked to provide support to Presbyterian or Methodist flocks scattered nearby, he willingly did so, either jumping onto his horse or walking to their parish, cheerfully on the lookout for quagga and elephant as he bundled down bridle paths spidery across the hills. Despite the family's hand-to-mouth existence and the questionable spiritual commitment of the Khoikhoi and a group then referred to as 'Fingoes' to the tenets of Christianity, there were glimpses of paradise. 'He [Barker] was also a keen gardener and planted black and white mulberries, as well as orange and peach trees, which he procured on his various journeys to Lombard's Post and elsewhere,' writes Stirk. 'He frequently rode down to the Kasouga river mouth with family, friends and visitors, where they bathed, rode along the beach and fished.'

While Barker survived the Khoikhoi's splendid indifference and the deluge of 1826, he didn't cope with the death of his wife. Ten years after the great, destructive flood, she died in childbirth and, with Long's help, we managed to track down her grave and at least one other. Colin came along with his dad, and the farmer's family trudged along with us. We parked the bakkies on the edge of the thicket and stumbled around for five minutes before finding the headstones. It was a strange moment, neither anticlimactic nor profound. It seemed the act of finding the graves was more important than thinking about them or trying to wrap our heads around what it all meant, because soon most of the party were heading back to open ground, perhaps too awkward to remain around the graves for long. As the main group departed, Jako and I found what we thought was probably the stillborn child's grave, listing hopelessly beneath a covering of leaves. We knelt down to make out the inscription, surmising that this was probably the Barkers' stillborn child, but weren't finally sure. We couldn't make out time's illegible scrawl.

Within two years Barker had left the mission, heading for the slightly more civilised confines of Paarl. He lived there for the rest of his life, remarrying and eventually becoming blind before he died in 1861. By moving to Paarl, Barker missed the disintegration of his beloved mission – and the action that took Gray's life. In 1851 a group of Khoikhoi men staying at the mission conspired to overthrow the station and return the land to the Xhosa. From what I can gather, the Theopolis economy was faltering. They had little water for irrigating crops and no lime (a scarcity throughout this section of the Cape Colony, according to Thomas Pringle), an important ingredient in concrete. Economic activity was confined to felling local trees for wagon parts and charcoal. Few crops survived the pestilence and rust, baptisms were down and morale was low after the death of Reverend Sass, Barker's successor. The religious vacuum and the prevailing harshness of the times forced some of the mission residents to look for alternative alliances and this is what led the Khoikhoi to kill some of their own before fleeing. News of the sedition reached the surrounding forts, while those who remained at Theopolis were evacuated under protection to Grahamstown. Under their leader, Kiewit Piqueur, the rebels made off with what they could, camping in the bush, and although some of them were killed in subsequent actions, others escaped to continue to harry Theopolis for another day. Gray was killed in one of many inconclusive skirmishes, as the rebels and their pursuers played a prolonged game of cat and mouse across the hills. It was the beginning of the end for Theopolis. Very soon it returned to dust.

We had lunch at the Pig 'n Whistle in Bathurst and discussed the controversial state of land reform. As we tucked into our burgers, Colin mentioned that government had appointed intermediaries to help new farmers find their way. It seemed like a wise initiative, although such cosy positions often went to the wrong people: farmers who had themselves failed at farming or those with little knowledge or empathy to offer. He spoke of a well-connected man down country who'd managed to finagle a farm through his political connections. The farm was once used for producing pineapples but that had long since ceased. It was marginal anyway, whether it had been repatriated or not. Perhaps it looked better on a spreadsheet of returned farms than it did in the flesh. Not for the first time on our walk through frontier country, I felt confused and depressed, aghast at the shallow predictability of it all.

After dropping off Jako at his parents' house in Kenton-on-Sea, we trundled back to Grahamstown. The rain we'd heard about – and successfully missed – began to flush down the Golf's windscreen. Close to the Salem turn-off we noticed a stationary car's hazard lights on the other side of the road and, in the middle of it, a man sitting down. We stopped and went across to him to find that he was not only hopelessly drunk, but uppity with it. Still mildly drunk ourselves, Craig and I grinned through his protestations and yanked him off the road, walking him to a ditch a couple of metres back. As we got back into the car, he sort-of abused us, kind-of thanked us, and we chuckled as we went on our way, darkness falling, the rain making us feel dry and warm inside the car. We hadn't got very far when we noticed in the rear-view mirror that he was up on his feet, swaying happily back down the road. We turned around, bundled him back into the car and went in search of the turn-off to home. We found it easily enough and put him on his way. The man, giggling as he lurched through the remaining light, seemed happier when we left him the second time. We felt quietly pleased with ourselves, Samaritans in the gloaming. It was a good way to end a memorable weekend.

3
THE MANY MAJESTIES OF THOMAS PRINGLE

---

*Driekop to the Eildon farmhouse, Baviaans River,
Eastern Cape — about 10 kilometres*

Spring had only just arrived when I left Johannesburg for my walk in Thomas Pringle country. Purple wisteria was curling around the columns of our stoep like smoke from a chimney, and from everywhere in our garden came the busy prod and restless nudge of life. In Grahamstown, where I had spent the week before the walk interviewing academics for the university's annual research report, winter was leaving in fits and starts. Although the flowers on the campus coral trees had mostly flamed open, the collection of stinkwoods in the quad overlooked by the English Department remained leafless, perhaps because they received no more than a tight-fisted ration of sun. These lichen-dusted trees, established and wise, somehow reminded me of cattle in a kraal, heads bowed, eyes droopy, lowing gently in the coming night.

Early on a fresh Saturday morning, the land still cold after almost a week of rain, Craig Paterson and I drove up to the Baviaans River Valley. There were fingers of mist in the drifts north of Grahamstown but as we got closer to Bedford the skies cleared and the day opened in a sun-swept flourish. We quickly skirted the grubby town and headed west for Cradock before finding a gravel road 13 kilometres further along. We were now heading north and after a climb onto higher land found ourselves following much the same route that Pringle's party of settlers had taken to get to their destination on the valley's upper reaches in the winter of 1820. What took us hours took them weeks. By day they marvelled and sweated as their wagons creaked northwards; by night, they shivered and fretted, listening to the roar and the rustle, cuddling close for comfort and warmth. 'We were pilgrims in the savage wilds of Africa,' wrote Pringle.

Having anchored offshore in Algoa Bay after a long trip from Gravesend (some say Greenwich) on the 400-ton frigate the *Brilliant*, the settlers eventually rode in longboats through the breakers and stuck fast on wet sand. Pringle wrote of the party's 'boisterous hilarity', of people who found their feet on solid ground for the first time in months, and it is easy to imagine wet clothes clinging to the body, the slap of the ocean and salty blaze of the sun, everywhere shouting and excitement, happiness and surprise. Although the scene was 'alive with bustle and confusion', the group's joys were short-lived. There was a muddle with accommodation, as the tents reserved for them had been occupied by another party, and they were asked to reboard the boats and temporarily head back to the *Brilliant*.

They returned a day or two later, provisioned kettles, hoes and seed on government credit, and commandeered oxen and wagons. Once supplied, they headed in a cradle roughly north-east, first to Uitenhage, from there to Grahamstown, after that across wildlife-abundant plains to Bedford. Pringle was eager to get moving, partly because his party wanted to see what awaited them, partly because he was sniffy about the quality of his fellow settlers. Staying behind on the beach when the rest of his party returned to the *Brilliant*, he looked about with a sour eye. 'Guessing vaguely from my observations on this occasion, and on subsequent rambles through their locations, I should say that probably about a third were persons of real respectability of character and possessed some worldly substance,' he wrote. 'But that the remaining two-thirds were for the most part composed of individuals of a very unpromising description – persons who had hung loose upon society – low in morals or desperate in circumstance.'

I imagined the landscape wasn't greatly different for Pringle's party of 24 from what it was for us, although kikuyu grass had been planted on the riverbanks in the 1950s, lending the landscape a bouncy Lake District lushness before the resumption of business-as-usual thorn and bush. There might have been a few more farms and greater habitation now; more rusty tractors, more bushes and more sheep. For the most part, though, the landscape was as it was then, now winter-parched, a dull palette of mute greens and drab browns, small green bushes obstinate on the hills, the river water the colour of weak drinking-chocolate.

Halfway up the valley we stopped at an old NG kerk, whitewashed and fading, like something out of the Texas panhandle in *Pat Garrett and Billy the Kid*. We swung open the heavy wooden door and nosed around. It was plain and forgotten, the main congregants a group of starlings with attention deficit disorder. We found our way to an ante-chamber behind the main nave and pulled back a curtain across a once-used fireplace. It was full of receipts in pastel colours, kindling for a fire that never was.

We nosed up the valley, keeping company with the river, scanning every bend for the farmhouse of Alex and Barrie Pringle, Thomas Pringle's descendants and owners of Eildon Farm. After maybe half an hour we found it, tucked behind a group of cypresses standing guard at the homestead. We followed a dry-stone wall and parked the car, introducing ourselves to a sprightly sixty-something couple. Alex was off for a round of Saturday golf at the Bedford Country Club, and Barrie would follow later to play tennis and make chicken pie with other wives and mothers for a club fundraiser that night. As we sat down to tea, Alex gave us a quick lesson in speed history, telling us the abbreviated story of the Pringle party's early years before leaving for his round. The party was made up in the main of Pringles and Rennies, he said, and they had trundled beyond where we were now to a point about 10 kilometres further up the valley called Camp's Drift. After being shown their meagre 40-hectare allocation by a kindly Afrikaner farmer, they attacked the land in a frenzy of industry, an emotion borne of disappointment and months of tedium aboard the *Brilliant*. They built dams, planted crops and orchards, and surrounded them with quince hedges. Unlike the English settlers – and this came from Thomas's writings rather than from Alex's story – they tended to eschew the ubiquitous wattle-and-daub houses, living instead in primitive, knocked-together structures. For them it was more important to tend their crops and usher the valley into life than to plaster the walls of their homes.

It was hard going. They suffered from drought, pestilence and locusts and, more gnawingly, from misery and loneliness. It didn't take them long to realise that the land was too marginal for apricots and wheat, the rainfall too flaky, and that they would be better served by herding sheep and goats, maybe a head or two of cattle if they could afford them. In the months that followed their failed attempts at farming, the group dispersed down the valley. Thomas's father, the patriarch, Robert, moved to Eildon with William Dodds, Thomas's half-brother, while Thomas spent time there writing poetry under the shade of a *witgat* tree, a gnarled, white-barked indigenous species with small leaves and a thick canopy. He lived in a beehive hut close to the tree and in these months fired South African poetry into life with his oddly sentimental poems about lion hunting, the Khoikhoi and the Xhosa people.

This was surely South African literature's Emersonian moment, calling to mind Ralph Waldo Emerson's essay on self-reliance and the need to find one's true, aboriginal self. 'A foolish consistency is the hobgoblin of little minds, adored by little statesmen and philosophers and divines,' wrote Emerson memorably. Under the *witgat*, Pringle strenuously asserted his native self, his individualism and view of the natural world. Despite being lame from an early age (he'd been dropped by a wet nurse while young, an accident that fractured his hip), Pringle was no slave to conformity. He was forever clearing his lungs, penning verse and letters, railing against injustice, an Emersonian in an Emersonian age. He was no slave to 'foolish consistency', indeed, just the opposite, forever stabbing a finger at authority's chest, insisting on his right to be heard. For all his forthright hectoring, he could be slyly manipulative. His writings tell of the terrible guilt felt by the wet nurse who dropped him as a child. When growing up he would work her guilt like bread dough, constantly shaping it to his wants and special needs.

An hour or two later, Craig and I were up on the farm's highest point, having been taken there by David, one of Alex and Barrie's four children. David had returned recently from a five-year stint as an accountant in Bermuda, and as we nudged onto higher ground in his bakkie, he told us the story of Mary Prince, a freed slave, born in Bermuda to a family of African descent. Prince had been the Pringles' housekeeper in Highgate, north London, where Thomas and his wife, Margaret Brown, had lived during the last years of his life. While in Bermuda, David had been contacted by a newspaper there, which, putting two and two together, had linked him back to the Pringles of the valley. At the time, Prince was being feted as a local heroine in Bermuda (where she was a symbol of national pluck and courage), and the paper sent round a reporter to interview him, taping him without his knowledge. As we were driving onto higher ground, opening and closing cattle gates along the way, David was less concerned about Bermudian newspaper ethics than he was about the hidden intrigues of Prince's story. As a freed slave, she had told her story to a ghost writer. With its depiction of sexual and physical cruelty, the book scandalised and titil-lated Regency England, and Prince became a figure of some renown. Contemporary accounts have pointed out, however, that Prince's 'autobiography' was massaged. She was depicted as sexually chaste, for example, because to portray her as sexually active would have diminished the sentimental tug of her story. What was the truth, the three of us wondered. Margaret was nine years older than Thomas and they never had children. Did Thomas and Mary have an affair, or were his care and kindness strictly platonic?

'He was slightly effeminate,' proferred Alex later, which led Craig and me to exchange knowing glances and save up the morsel for some juicy gossip in the car back to Grahams-town. We both wondered if this was Alex's way of sidling up to the idea that Pringle was gay.

Once David left us on high land with directions back to the Eildon farmhouse, we stepped into the grandest of days. Eildon is a big farm – 10 000 morgen – and we were dropped on Driekop, the farm's highest point, winding gradually downwards through a gentle switchback of knuckles to the farmhouse door. There wasn't a cloud in the sky and every-where the hills were dusted with bitter Karoo, a kind of yellow-green heather that gave the hillocks a perky radiance, bright against the blue of the sky. There were great pillows of it everywhere, softly inviting, playgrounds sometimes broken by a single thorn tree but usually just sweeping bountifully through the grass, sometimes brown, sometimes bursting into the moist green of springtime. The bitter Karoo patches seemed to follow no logic that we could see, except, perhaps, for a sense of where to find subterranean water. You'd look up or look across at a nearby crest and there the bitter Karoo would be, great flags of it draped across the midday hills like washing in the sun.

At first we didn't notice the other signs of growth but, beginning to look more carefully, we noticed yellow and mauve daisies strewn across the hills and grass tinged with the crisp, fragile, new green of springtime. Enjoying ourselves now that we were out of a car and walking, pulling clean air into our lungs and sucking in the landscape, we noticed a warthog trotting along a contour path opposite as we came off Driekop to lower ground. I couldn't quite reconcile the warthog's obvious cheekiness with David's request about whether I'd like to shoot one – I declined politely – and realised they weren't held in high regard. Alex called them vermin, and they were shot on sight. 'They don't respect fences,' he said. 'They push right through. We lose 40 per cent of our lambing flock to vermin annually. Until 1989 there wasn't a jackal in this part of the world and then they were reintroduced. Jackals and warthogs are our biggest single problem – we've tried everything.'

As our eyes became sensitive to the subtleties of the landscape, we noticed pools linked by no more than a sludgy trickle that were full of tadpole spawn, busy clouds of it, seething in the shallows like living jam. Each time we approached a pool for a better view, we'd hear plopping in front of us, as frogs scrambled for cover. What prevents frogs from behaving more obligingly? Some secret code of frog honour, or just general perversity? They seem to jump from under the very sole of your boot as it comes down, yet invariably escape without revealing themselves. You know they're close by – and sometimes catch a blur of comic terror – but they never linger, always heading for depths and shadows. I remember spending long happy minutes watching bullfrogs at our local mall when Thomas, the third of our sons, was younger. In between two arms of the mall was an outdoor putt-putt course, with a rockery and water features. On Friday nights in summer we occasionally took to the course, pleading with our balls to run over the crest *towards* the hole and not achingly backwards towards us. With teeth-clenching effort, I concentrated on 'pocking' my ball over the bump or avoiding the water feature and, in the interests of peace, tried not to be too bothered by Thomas's cheating, his sevens and eights converted blithely downwards into competitive fours and fives. We usually followed our 18 holes up with a burger and chips at the on-course takeaway, laughing as we added up our cards to see who'd won. The best part of the day was at the end of the meal, when we found a tucked-away pool free of putt-putt traffic and watched frogs sing and glide. They were *rustig* here, at easy leisure, comfortable with humans. As is the way of life in cities, I didn't think about the frogs for months, and the next time we went back for putt-putt, the course was closed and the water feature dried up, the bullfrog orchestra no more.

* * *

Pringle's Britain was a seething potjie, brought to the boil by the radical updrafts sweeping through Europe as a result of the Napoleonic Wars. It was fanned by class antagonism and textile-worker anxiety – particularly in the north of England – as well as a generalised feeling of being hard done by, particularly for the poor. Famine was commonplace, unemployment rife, and social inequality widespread. While life for the poor was physically grim, it was also spiritually and existentially absurd. The Corn Laws, for example, imposed high tariffs on the importation of corn, despite thousands starving. And democracy? That was an elaborate sham. Voting was restricted to adult men who were owners of the freehold and tended to be more widespread in the south of England than the north. In Scotland, the Pringles' home, all 45 Scottish MPs owed their seats to patronage, and there was a clear gulf between the voters and their elected officials, and those looking in on the cosy world of sherry parties and horse-drawn traps. Constituency boundaries were frequently outdated, so much so that parliamentarians could sometimes be elected by a handful of voters – the so-called 'rotten boroughs' – with voting only being allowed by vocal and very public declarations at the hustings. Seldom had the social edifice creaked quite as much.

Much of this social ferment culminated in the Peterloo Massacre of August 1819, when a large group of disenfranchised workers gathered on St Peter's Field in Manchester to demand parliamentary reform. The group, estimated to be between 60 000 and 80 000 strong, gathered to listen to a speech by Henry Hunt of the Manchester Patriotic Union. Known as 'the orator', Hunt had a well-known reputation for rabble-rousing and the authorities became jittery. The cavalry were called in. They drew their sabres and charged the mob, killing 15 and injuring hundreds more. The name 'Peterloo' was an ironic reference to the Battle of Waterloo, four years previously, and even though the event gave rise to the birth of the *Manchester Guardian*, opinion is divided over the effectiveness of the meeting or the willingness of the authorities to listen carefully to the clamour of the hungry. For potential emigrants, though, a sliver of hope. Nicholas Vansittart, Chancellor of the Exchequer, secured £50 000 to promote a scheme of emigration to the Cape Colony shortly afterwards. If the government couldn't deal with unrest at home, it was reasoned, they would simply ship some of the agitators and urban distressed abroad. As it was, Vansittart's initiative was wildly oversubscribed. Of 90 000 applications, 5 000 were chosen, among them the Pringles of Kelso, Roxburghshire, in the border country of southern Scotland.

Pringle was the third son in a large Scottish family of tenant farmers. Although they had no vote (because they didn't own the land on which they lived), they were *bywoners* with a difference: they had attitude. They were pious and aspirational, disinclined to accept the careless wisdoms of the day. The simmering tensions of contemporary Britain weren't lost on them, and when Thomas read about the Cape emigration scheme in the *Caledonian Mercury* in July 1819, a seed was planted. They would catch a boat south from Leith and ship out to the colonies. They could own land and worship in their own church, eat food from their own garden. Here was the opportunity for freedom and self-sufficiency, a fresh fashioning in a new land. According to the Public Records

Office in Kew, London, there were so-termed 'agriculturalists' in the Pringle party's midst, bakers and ploughmen. Thomas had worked as a clerk in Edinburgh and found, almost mystically, that he could charm words from his fountain pen. He could think and sustain an argument. They pooled a little capital and they had a little nous; they would be fine.

Despite the attractions of the scheme, Pringle wasn't blinded by the pufferies of contemporary salesmanship. He looked at the world of men with his keen naturalist's eye and harrumphed: 'A sort of utopian delirium was somehow excited at that time in the public mind about South Africa,' he wrote in *Some Account of the Present State of the English Settlers in Albany, South Africa*. 'And the flowery descriptions of superficial observers seem to have been intoxicated with their Circean blandishments, not merely the gullible herd of uninformed emigrants, but many sober men, both in and out of parliament.' Still, the Pringles paid their money and made the voyage, joining the motley ranks of the uninformed as they battled with seasickness, scurvy and boredom.

It was difficult to be intoxicated by the world into which the Pringle party was dropped because it was wild, barren and full of dispersed tensions. The Slagtersnek rebellion had happened in the vicinity only five years before the party arrived and the countryside had its fair share of prickly Boers with a wagonload of grievance. The Boers generally hated the British, the British were mistrustful of the Boers, the Khoikhoi and the Xhosa, and everyone was suspicious of everyone else. Despite the gripe and the toil, Alex told us that the farmers hereabouts had been kind to the Pringle party. This was generally underpopulated land (one of the reasons for the lack of land claims in the area, said Alex), which meant that people recognised the need for friendship and mutual reliance. Not that this was always the case. The Slagtersnek rebellion came about because the authorities became *gatvol* with the careless dispensing of local justice by a group of *hardebaard* Boers called the Bezuidenhouts, and the Pringles would soon have become aware of who lined up where and who could be trusted. Thomas Pringle was the classic observer – you see it in his writings, always leaving a part of himself and his deformity outside the dusty swirl of the everyday. He watched and recorded and composed. And here we were, walking where he had walked and looking at pretty much what he would have looked at.

Although maybe it wasn't quite this neat. There is, for example, a Thomas Baines artwork hanging in the Pringles' lounge. It was painted from a vantage point roughly south-west of the current homestead, on one of the gravel roads that we had walked along in the late afternoon after coming off the mountain, our boots and socks just dusty enough to suggest a proper walk. Clipping through cattle pens and the odd kraal, Craig dragging on his cigarette, we spotted electricity pylons and so knew civilisation was round the next bend. On the last stretch, we walked along one of several of the farm's carefully maintained canals and soon found ourselves on the edge of the farm's biggest dam, trying to avoid the endless swarms of insects and flies. When we discussed the Baines painting, both David and Alex mentioned that they'd never quite been able to locate the point from which it had been painted. They had walked outward along the road, turned and looked backwards, but still couldn't quite pinpoint where Baines had put his easel. Such was the quest of the families in the valley to locate their history, pinning down the wings of the past for careful and regular examination. Maybe there was a simple explanation for the Baines painting. It might have been composed from memory, or was perhaps a composite of views, something figurative rather than something naturalistic, an approximation that didn't recognise the deliberate inaccuracies and therefore the artifice of its own making.

Back home, I looked at Baines' colonial landscapes on the internet. *The Battle of Blaauwkrantz* caught my eye and it was only then that I realised I'd seen it before. As a boy, my paternal grandmother, Elsie, made me scrapbooks. I don't quite know why, but it was presumably to encourage my reading and interest me in the wider world. I remember black-and-white *Eastern Cape Herald* photographs of the great Port Elizabeth flood of 1969, showing wash-aways and torrents, the city's Christmas lights and decorations strangely cheerful amidst the ruin. There were colour images of Frik du Preez – how I loved that Springbok jersey – bounding downfield, the ball gripped in a single massive hand. There was also a large colour reproduction of the Baines painting. As a seven- or eight-year-old, I looked at it with a child's innocence. I didn't see the sentimentality or the bigger political picture. I simply saw a group of trekboers defending their oxwagon, men with billowing shirts open to the navel, strangely cherubic children trying to fire pistols. They were surrounded by a group of Zulu impis in caracul skins advancing towards them with assegais. Looking at it again today and I realise that the painting is a cautionary tale, a moral fable about the tribal propensity for terror. All I remember from seeing it as a child was that it scared me shitless.

* * *

There was a great desire on the farm to polish the past so it caught the light. There were maps and artefacts and photographs, some of them enchanting, everywhere markers leading back to the original claim. As we were left to the run of the house that evening, Alex and Barrie heading off to the Bedford Club for a meal with their mates, we had ample opportunity to have a good look at them all. I most enjoyed the old black-and-white framed photographs of the Port Elizabeth wool sheds, in which fleeces from Eildon were baled. They showed bearded men in black suits standing in massive harbour warehouses. The bales are nearly stacked to the ceiling, so stuffed with wool that it constantly peeps out of messy corners like old-fashioned upholstery in a torn car seat. Alex told us that the early 1950s was a boom time for the international wool price, with the spike in demand being caused by the US stockpiling the commodity during the Korean War. For a year or two, wool prices in Australia, South Africa and New Zealand went through, in a manner of speaking, the warehouse roof. Prices were never as good again and had been declining steadily ever since. The destination for the wool had also changed. Alex told us that prices for quality goat's wool were best in Italy and China. He added

73

that this year's roving crew of workers were about to come in and spend a week or two shearing the goat and sheep flock in a shed built with the profits from the original boom.

This will to history, the desire to retain and therefore keep alive one's past, was given its most pointed expression in the 1960s and 70s. During this time, many settler descendants in the greater region, not only in the valley, felt that the circuits of power were lighting up for the Nationalists, and not for them. As a result, this became a self-conscious time of rediscovering settler identity, a general flexing of muscle in response to official neglect. The 1820 Settlers' National Monument was built during this period, and Tom Barker, the Member of Parliament for Grahamstown and Albany, was an enthusiastic champion of the settler cause. A stone church was built on Eildon from local stone in 1957 and it was always the intention to repatriate Pringle's remains from Bunhill Fields in London, where he was buried along with literary giants, like William Blake, Daniel Defoe and John Bunyan. The return took a surprisingly long time but money was found and favours called in. Thomas Pringle was brought 'home' to a place that was no more than an important way station on his life's journey. 'We heard that a highway was about to be built through Bunhill Fields and the entire graveyard destroyed,' Alex told me. 'We'd wanted to get back Thomas's remains anyway. We had a few contacts at Safmarine and phone calls were made. Eventually, to cut a long story short, we had the body exhumed and transported back to the farm and buried in the crypt in 1971.'

The following day I visited the church – small, solitary and sparsely beautiful. It stands in a field, with a pine tree or two nearby, adjacent to the gravel road through the valley, and looks slightly incongruous but is no less captivating for that. According to Alex, it cost £6 000 to build, a considerable sum in those days, and is clean and bright with pride. Family weddings and local funerals are held here, and I found it difficult not to be moved as I ran my hand across the wooden pews and read the inscription to Pringle's grave helpfully fastened to the wall, the original inscription in Bunhill Fields having become corroded to illegible scratches: '... In the walks of British literature he was known as a man of genius; in the domestic circle he was loved as an affectionate relative and faithful friend; in the wide sphere of humanity he was revered as the advocate and protector of the oppressed; he left among the children of the African desert a memorial of his philanthropy; and bequeathed to his fellow-countrymen an example of enduring virtue. Having lived to witness the cause in which he had ardently and energetically laboured, triumph in the emancipation of the Negro, he himself was called from the bondage of the world.'

The Pringle party was not only distressed at having to farm on marginal lands, they were also lonely. It was the colonial authorities' intention to ship two more parties of Scots out to Baviaans River, but neither made the voyage successfully. One group, under Captain Grant, plumped to go to Canada instead, the second suffered a terrible fire aboard their transport ship, the *Abeona*, which sank. The Pringles and Rennies, therefore, had to make do with each other and their Khoikhoi retainers for company. Thomas chafed at it all, voyaging through the Albany district as he made a case for the authorities' thoughtlessness, using his disappointment as the dynamo to power his pen. Before long, the bloodlust of the lion hunt began to fade. He hooked up with his old mate, John Fairbairn, in Cape Town, and the two started periodicals and short-lived newspapers. Pringle's barbs and arrows didn't take long to prick Lord Charles Somerset's exceptionally thin skin. The governor of the colony didn't take kindly to the criticism of himself and his officer son, and it didn't take long before Pringle had left the Cape for London. An inveterate activist and joiner of causes, he became an influential member of the abolitionist movement, may or may not have had sexual relations with his housemaid, Mary Prince, and succumbed to tuberculosis aged 45. He strove for intellectual and creative wealth throughout an adventurous life, but in the end perished to the ultimate poor man's disease.

Alex, however, provided a nice antidote to the cult of Pringle. He clearly loved the idea of the Pringle past and the Pringle farm, yet wasn't so enamoured with the cult that he couldn't see around its edges. It was he who gently floated the idea that Pringle was gay, and it was David who talked slyly about Pringle's possible extramarital relations with Mary Prince. Alex was of the view that Pringle wasn't as liberal as he was made out to be. He was something of a secret agent, a critic from within, but knew exactly where his community began and where it ended. Alex didn't say so in so many words, but, thinking about it afterwards, Pringle's lameness and Scottishness clearly played a part in allowing him to stand at an angle to the English pieties of the day. Pringle invariably took the contrary view, yet could never be branded a radical. Such a view initiated a tradition in South Africa of English poetry, a tradition that flowed towards Roy Campbell and Douglas Livingstone, through Patrick Cullinan, and onwards towards Mike Nicol and Stephen Watson. He might even have been the unintended creator of a broader, more vital spring – the secular liberal humanism of, say, Alan Paton, although this is not what he'll finally be remembered for.

It seemed the best critics, then, of the Pringle myth were the Pringles themselves. It was an exceedingly good position to occupy because you could both celebrate and deconstruct, sometimes simultaneously. One of the disadvantages of having Pringle as a virtual tenant, however, was that you thought about him all the time. It allowed you to make and remake the myth, shaping either gently or more forcefully as the opportunity arose. With the 200th anniversary of the settlers' arrival approaching, my guess is that the Pringle myth might go through more iterations. Some will boost the name, others will pick again at the bones of the known. I was simply happy to have been here, to have visited, and have been welcomed as a guest. The family's generosity was remarkable. Craig and I couldn't have asked for more.

The following morning we visited Ernest Pringle, the clan's mildly eccentric outlier, collector of this and that, and purveyor of frank, state-of-the-nation opinions. We'd been briefed – Ernest had strong views on land restitution and consulted for Agri SA – and were apprehensive that we might get swept into a political argument about 'the blacks' or cadre deployment or land-reform idiocy, one of those tiresomely white South African discussions that proceed benignly enough until they suffocate you with assumptions about 'us' and 'them'. We've all been there before: suddenly, because you haven't been vigilant or assertive enough, you find that you're stuck fast in the coils of racism, having the political life squeezed out of you, sentence by bigoted sentence. You end up hating yourself for the rest of the day, thinking that you're a political coward and conflict-averse, and would like yourself more if you could simply find a way of telling whoever you are talking to at the braai or dinner party or family reunion that, for you, politics aren't quite so absolute. Neither, for that matter, now you come to think of it, is life. But you don't say any of this. You bite your lip and invariably regret it.

Perhaps because he was more careful than we gave him credit for, Ernest, a ruddy, curly-haired man in boots and pressed shorts, guided us through his twin collections of butterflies and farm artefacts without fuss. There was no political argument, nothing quite as crass as trying to get us on side. Housed in a shadowy outhouse, the artefacts were what you might find in a provincial museum, once a local commercial centre but since bypassed by the new national road. There were old rifles and road signs, bandoliers and farm implements, some golf clubs, possibly even some small animal skeletons. There was even an old post-office bag of scuffed leather, the ultimate expression of times lost, when the Post Office was still a functioning entity and black labourers kneaded their hands and looked at their shoes when addressed by the *grootbaas*. Ernest told us with what I think was nostalgia that the bag was from hereabouts. It had been tossed into a drum or simply thrown onto a roadside verge awaiting collection. The service was so reliable that his father could write to him as a boarder in St Andrew's in Grahamstown and receive a reply in the next cycle of mail a day or two later.

We poked about disconsolately, not wanting to appear rude. I tried to link what I was seeing to a story or bigger picture but failed miserably. I felt buttonholed and ill at ease, and would have liked to have been left alone to reflect on what I was seeing in silence. After about 10 minutes of excessive politeness, Ernest pulled out from a shelf at our feet some Khoisan scrapers and thick, bagel-shaped stones. These are called bored stones, and were used to add weight to digging sticks, the stone being threaded through their hollow middle until it caught tight on a crook or slight thickening of the shaft. The sticks to which they added weight were put to a variety of uses, including digging pits for game capture and hacking open termite mounds. They were also used in ceremonial functions, and for *muti*. Sometimes hides or skins would be beaten with these sticks to bring rain or luck in the hunt. They surely – and this is my pet theory rather than any archaeological wisdom – would also have been used to mark or write or annotate, a form of primitive stylus or pen. Perhaps they were also used for water divination or simple comfort? For there is nothing as profoundly reassuring as the feel of wood or stone in the warmth of your hands, after all.

It struck me afterwards that these simple Stone Age implements went back further than we could ever imagine. We were seeing a rare chink of light from beneath a door. These were artefacts used by hunter-gatherers who lived in this valley tens of thousands of years ago. They woke with the dawn and watched the sky for clouds; they scanned the hills for game and were vaguely and inarticulately comforted by the river's restless beauty. They were older than Pringle's *witgat*; older, too, than his poems and his chest thumping. Baines, with his view-that-could-not-be-fathomed, was a mere transient, a callow ideologue, a man who painted not out of the need to discover but a desire to confirm in painterly form what everyone already knew. Savages, ran the Baines worldview, were savage; colonial landscapes were beautiful, terrifying and terrifyingly beautiful, their apparent emptiness an invitation to mine and fence and pillage. By showing us the stones, Ernest, perhaps inadvertently, perhaps by soft design, had offered us a glimpse of the great timeless lyric of our land. It was a time before settlement and settlers, before poetry, before the cult of Pringle and the imperialist propaganda of Baines, a time before the bright noise of the chattering classes, people liable to confuse opinions with wisdom and arguments with knowledge. The time of stones is a time, I think, for which we have only notional regard any more.

4
PEREIRA OF PATON COUNTRY

Carisbrooke via Stainton to Ixopo — about 12 kilometres

Alan Paton not only had a feel for a snugly crafted novel, he also had an eye for the natural drama of the unusual view. The opening sequences of his 1948 novel, *Cry, the Beloved Country*, are set at Carisbrooke siding, where, famously, the grass-covered hills 'are lovely beyond any singing of it'. Even today, the hills beyond the meagre siding remain softly inviting, mildly green after poor summer rains, forever rolling. Taking in this very view as he waits for his narrow-gauge train, it is from here that the character of the Reverend Stephen Kumalo travels to Stainton, Ixopo and Donnybrook before boarding the midnight thunder to Johannesburg. He has been summoned, for the big city has swallowed his son, Absalom, and sister, Gertrude. Reluctantly, he must go in search of them and shepherd them home.

After being dropped at Carisbrooke one mild, misty Saturday in November, my wife and I were advised to walk up the hill behind the siding by Julian Pereira, our guide for the weekend. Julian is an agriculturalist by training but a huckster by preference, a jolly, energetic, unselfconscious man who loves the countryside in which he lives and is surprisingly reverential towards Paton's novel. He's spent the last 15 years collecting narrow-gauge track and rusted tin houses for the station at Allwoodburn in Ixopo. The Paton's Country Railway initiative (whose track we were about to walk along) is due to his persistence and crafty opportunism.

Pereira might not have imagined that his future would wind through the hills of his life in quite this way. He talked to us of fighting NUSAS students in the 70s, manning the Dusi Bridge with his mates in Pietermaritzburg armed with hockey sticks because they wanted to be left alone to continue their studies without lefty agitation. He's been a rural advisor to the Department of Agriculture, a pig farmer, and has dabbled in computers and laying down lines for a local network. His most recent heist was to lever two rare General Electric diesel locomotives from the Transnet workshops in Port Elizabeth and bring them to Ixopo on the back of two flatbed trucks. He had schmoozed a representative of the then KwaZulu-Natal premier, Senzo Mchunu's office to wrest them away from Port Elizabeth, where they would possibly have ended up hauling the Apple Express train, saying that the local tourist initiative couldn't do without them, and lubricated his argument by plying him with home-brewed orange wine. The wine must've been good because Pereira received his locomotives quicker than he'd expected, a quick word here and a phone call there speeding matters along. His latest gambit in bringing the wider world to Carisbrooke was to build a glass theatre opposite the siding on the lip of the valley. 'We're going to do a Paton musical with music by

Andrew Lloyd Webber,' he announced, eyes bright. 'The tourists will love it.'

After he left us, we followed his advice and climbed the hill behind the siding. The haul was wet and slippery but once on the tableland up above, there were fine views west towards Umzimkhulu sprawling down in the valley, the cloud-obscured peaks of Mount Currie and what was once called the 'no-man's-land' of East Griqualand beyond. We ran our hands along the rough edges of a trig beacon, its pole collapsed through rust, and tried to make out from where exactly the sound of children's close but faraway voices was coming. Kumalo's train comes from the direction of Umzim-khulu, chugging through mist, past aloes and thick fields of cane. The novel tells us that if you listen carefully to the train's whistle you might know where it is, alongside which farm, what river: 'But though Stephen Kumalo has been there a full hour before he need, he does not listen to these things. This is a long way to go and a lot of money to pay ... and Johannesburg is a great city, with so many streets they say that a man can spend his days going up one and down another, and never the same one twice.'

Once we'd seen the views and listened to the children's voices without finding them, we switch-backed down the hill's flank, our shoes and boots greasy with a high tide of mud. It was a lovely morning, recent-rain fresh, and we followed the tracks towards Ixopo, first walking through 'the dim wall of wattles', as described in the book, soon pushing on to where the walls alternately changed to indigenous hard-wood, then back to man-planted forest. Every so often quickly

83

arriving views presented themselves: a glimpse of rondavel huts with mauve walls dotted on a distant hillside, sometimes small birds of prey. There were crows, loose-winged and louche, messengers from the underworld, with their sinister cry. I noticed a buck, a duiker perhaps, that had wandered in between the tracks, and called Lisa over. By the time we looked again it had disappeared, sprite-like, from view. A little further along we saw an almost-white pig, rooting around in the moist earth as it walked across the sometimes rusty, sometimes slick rails, unhurried as a country parson.

The walking was neither difficult nor easy. Lisa chose to walk in between the tracks, the spacing of the sleepers ideal for the length of her step. I walked alongside the rails. It was mostly straightforward, sometimes uneven and more challenging. By walking the tracks, she missed the culverts. I plunged down the one side, jogging up the next. At times, feeling lazy, I joined her back on the tracks. They were somehow lazy too. Everything seemed considered and gradual in the quiet provided by the incessant avenues of evenly spaced trees. No curve was ever hastily attempted. Gradients rose so subtly that had we not taken Julian's locomotive ride the following day, we wouldn't even have been aware that we were going up an incline. While pottering about on the edge of the tracks – the bed of stones on which they were supported was uneven – I fell. It wasn't a dangerous fall, I didn't hurt myself badly, but it was face-first and superbly undignified. I tore a chunk out of the fleshy bit of my hand as I broke my fall and cut my knee. Mostly, though, I felt stupid. Lisa ministered and made it better, dabbing my hand with toilet paper and then wrapping it in the cellophane that covered our avos, all the first-aid supplies we had. The grazes stung and I laughed at my stupidity, consoling myself with the fact that at least we weren't on our first date.

It was Lisa who usually fell. She had fallen in the Fens, years ago, one of our first breaks after having arrived to live and work in London. We were surrounded by fields of rape, yellow like Vincent van Gogh's sunflowers, and canals whose surface water was ruffled by the wind, the faraway blur of a lock keeper's cottage off in the distance. Bounding along, she had twisted her ankle and, pushed down by a decently weighted pack, plunged onto the boardwalk like a deadweight. I feared she had smashed her nose. Then there was the infamous 'Prijepolje incident'. We were either looking for a monastery or for our hotel, and she was tired. Suddenly she twisted her ankle and went down in abject surrender. We hobbled over to the hotel, a Stalinist bunker without a guest in sight. The lifts didn't work and there was moss growing in the stairwell (you could see it because the bannisters were made of glass). We eventually made it to our room and I tried to make her comfortable. Her ankle had swollen to the size of a tennis ball and she hurt all over. Her pride was damaged and we were hungry and homesick. I fried potatoes in our little room and added yoghurt, garlic and paprika. We ate as though we had never tasted food and christened the meal 'Potatoes Prijepolje'. When she smiled I knew we might just make it to the local bus depot, which basically amounted to taking a rickety bus driven by a death-seeking driver to the next undersupplied Serbian or Kosovan town.

Throughout our travels in the former Yugoslavia it was moot as to who was poorer – us or the country at large. I remember sharing a campsite in Kosovo with a cool couple from California. They were bicycling around Europe, and were tanned and lithe and friendly. It was strange waking in the middle of the night to hear small-arms fire in the mountains. We'd worry about it for a while, look at each other fearfully and drift back to sleep. In the morning we'd head for the ablution block and realise that it was just the four of us, singing R.E.M songs as we brushed our teeth. The Serbian military had commandeered the local high school as a barracks because ethnic Albanians trapped in Kosovo close to the Albanian border were getting cocky. We realised that at some point all of this was likely to blow but found ourselves strangely transfixed. There was a potential Hemingway moment in this faraway Balkan pocket, and the restless adventurer in me wanted to hang out. If we were lucky, we might even be witness to a nasty little war?

If we weren't visiting mosques and monasteries, admiring the tiles and the calm stateliness of the minarets, we were rummaging around for supplies in the local shops. It boiled down to tomatoes, cucumbers, bread and milk. We had a little money – not much – but there was nothing to buy. Eventually it was time to forego this faraway slice of Kosovo and make for the bright lights of Sarajevo. We would try not to fight on the bus trip there. I was hopelessly young and neurotic, worried that Lisa, an attractive Danish blonde, would be kidnapped by some hot-blooded Turk. That was when she wasn't falling flat on her face, of course, which did nothing, I reminded myself, to enhance her sex appeal to sundry Balkan Lotharios. I wasn't being mindlessly jealous. We'd been in Turkey at the start of our trip, then in Greece, before catching the train from Thessaloniki to Skopje, in Macedonia. In southern Turkey a local had fallen in love with her. He was love-smitten and desperately forward. He even took her out for a moonlight drive – on his tractor. I stayed behind in our room, reading a book, veering between being coolly unconcerned and laughing hysterically.

When Turkish men weren't showing a healthy appreciation of my girlfriend's bum by either pinching or slapping it, we were being stalked. We'd been told to approach Istanbul by sea, so we caught an overland bus with faulty air conditioning to Izmir, and from there took a brief but hazardous night-time journey by *dolmus* to Izmit. It was on the second bus that Zeki Arbeki sidled up to us, although, to be more accurate, it was Lisa to whom he presented his halitosis-wracked, exuberantly cheery self. We were mildly alarmed to find that Zeki was getting off where we got off and, strange this, discovered that he had the very idea we did – to approach the spires of the great city by ferry – which required him to move in to the same hotel. We were now getting slightly spooked. Lisa had given Zeki her address back in Cape Town and here we were, in a budget hotel on the Sea of Marmara, waiting to take the morning ferry to Istanbul with a friend we didn't want. Come dinnertime on the eve of the trip, we crept down a fire escape rather than pass him idling in reception. When we hauled our rucksacks onto the ferry the following morning, we did so sure in the knowledge that we had finally given him the slip, but there he was, smiling, as Lisa and I exchanged panicked glances. Strangely, on the voyage into Istanbul Zeki seemed hurt, like a dog kicked once too often. He clearly wasn't his usual bullish, let-me-invade-your-body-space kind-of self, and we felt almost guilty to have punctured his overtures so cruelly. When the ferry docked at the quay we bowled down the gangplank with our packs and found our way to the Hotel Munchen, leaving Zeki behind. I found the going difficult. Trying to read the map, negotiate the traffic and form a one-man cordon sanitaire around Lisa's derriere was immensely challenging. Years later Lisa still received an occasional letter with a Turkish stamp, redirected from her childhood Bergvliet address to wherever we happened to be staying in London. She tore them up and wondered who Zeki was stalking now.

After threading our way through the fairy-tale forests outside of Carisbrooke siding we stopped for lunch, eating our salami-and-cheese sandwiches in fine rain. I sipped tea with my thumb in the air and tried not to be reminded of my gashed hand and wounded pride. The walk had started through a grotto of young wattles, spines straight, thin leaves light on the sometimes rusted track. For a while we walked roughly parallel to the R56, heading to Umzimkhulu through the trees to our left but, almost without noticing it, we had changed direction, leaving the sweep of noisy trucks and cars behind. After lunch the views opened up. We chuffed into Stainton, a ghost siding, with clunky switching apparatus as the track briefly broke in two. The was a concrete sign that said 'Stainton', like a banner suspended between two poles, and a maturing plane tree on a mop of grass in the middle distance signalling the final leg into Ixopo. The tree was so close to the tracks that I imagined that little boys could reach out from the carriage windows and touch its white bark or engage it in passing conversation. It was young, with apple-green leaves, and stood with pleasing poise, reminding me of those rare Free State towns where the trans-Karoo trains once used to steam down the main street.

Further along and the forestry workers were coming to the end of their half-day Saturday shifts, a converted, slightly tubby white truck parked in a siding waiting to transport them back to Ixopo. Some workers with orange goggles and hard hats ran to catch it; others preferred to walk back to town on puddled forestry roads. As we walked past them in a wide arc, we noticed mirth in the air, the banter and chatter of achieved leisure and shebeen afternoons, cigarette smoke and ribaldry. We were shouted at good-naturedly and shouted back, doffing our hats in greeting. Beyond the changing forestry workers were large swathes of cleared forest, the stacked wattles and blue gums fanning out like so many matchsticks in the distance. We walked happily, sometimes through ferns, sometimes through weeds. The going was easy. My hand felt better. Sometimes you could smell eucalyptus resin on the washed air. It was peaceful and lulling and still, a lovely day for walking.

* * *

Early in *Cry, the Beloved Country*, the Reverend Stephen Kumalo tells a seemingly innocuous lie. He brags to his fellow passengers on the train to Jozi that this is a trip he has made countless times, although we suspect otherwise. There is something touching about Kumalo's untruth because it is the fib of a younger man – a braggart trying to impress a girl he fancies – and seems somehow inappropriate for an ageing reverend. In a more nuanced way, the lie is gently suggestive of his ill-formed craving for a different relationship with Absalom, his estranged son. Had he overcome his reluctance to visit the dangerous city, he would have been closer to Absalom; he might even have managed to save him from the horrible fate that awaited him. The lie initiates a counter-factual, fashioning the world with the endless 'what ifs' of regret.

By its very nature, a lie is a slippery spiritual and ontological fish. It is paradoxical, for as a fundamental untruth, something that is meant to foreclose because wrong, lies are sinisterly creative – they open up new paths and vistas, alternative realities. Kumalo's lie is enabling in a whole variety of ways but, most importantly, it gives him the cladding of humanness so many of Paton's other characters so obviously lack. While most of them plod like so many soapstone pieces across the board, Kumalo's lie makes him bristle with something vital. Paton's other characters are empty, echo chambers for his political and sociological beliefs, whereas Kumalo writhes with life force because of his lie. It is not insignificant that the lie occurs early on in the novel and is returned to later, with Kumalo reflecting on it in a bothered, gnawing-at-a-bone kind of way. Paton wants us to notice the Reverend Stephen Kumalo's culpability in his son's fate. If he had been a more assertive father, life for Absalom might have turned out differently and the double tragedy of two fathers both losing their sons might have been avoided.

It is this tragic element – the tragedy of two fathers, neighbours and strangers, alienated through circumstance, both losing their sons – that makes *Cry, the Beloved Country* such a powerful novel. I reread the book's final pages on a flight down to Port Elizabeth, surrounded by a brigade of late-middle-aged German tourists. They had been yacking about the leisurely way in which the baggage handlers were approaching their task and I felt quickly self-righteous, listening to their comments, watching their nods of the head and snide laughter as they observed the ground staff through their cabin windows. Eventually, with the baggage stowed, we took off, leaving them to their Sudoku and long wrestle with the *Frankfurter Allgemeine Zeitung* crossword. Breathing more freely as I dug in to my seat, I paged my way through the book's horrible conclusion, where the Reverend Stephen Kumalo heaves his old body onto the mountain to pray and Absalom, a strangely hapless victim of a system that has forsaken him, is hanged at first light.

As I read, I found myself crying, quiet, self-conscious tears trickling down my cheeks. The ending is so sad, Absalom so young and unfulfilled, the minor black characters' victimhood so eternal, that it is difficult not to recognise the suffering and injustice. Not that the ending is without hope. Milk comes to Kumalo's parish and Jarvis's grandson brings his perky innocence. Dams are built and the church roof is repaired, so, indirectly, Absalom's sacrifice brings a better life for all. Paton has been artful in his manipulation of the

Absalom character, keeping him away from us until he needs to emerge. At first he has simply been difficult to find, the idea being that this might be an almost-benign disappearance common in large cities. Then we become aware that there is something more disturbing about Absalom's address-hopping. After that comes the inevitable realisation that despite his progress in the reformatory, Absalom is a *tsotsi* and, in all likelihood, has been involved in the Parkwold murder. With Absalom spending so much time waiting in the wings, Paton risks the accusation that he is the expression of a sociological possibility (the strong chance that young men from the rural hinterland might be corrupted by the city) rather than a fully fledged character. On reflection, it is not Absalom for whom I cried, because Absalom has neither flesh nor personality. As a father of three beautiful sons, I cried for the reverend, because he grappled and failed to be a father worthy of *his* son.

One can, of course, cry during a Hollywood rom-com while knowing full well that the film is never going to enter the pantheon of great movies. In much the same way, it's not difficult to identify what is wrong with Paton's novel. His characters, for example, are crude, his action clumsy, his dialogue so excruciatingly formal that it is inadvertently funny. Despite this, the book fills us with its great, sentimental pathos, animated in part by the terrible backstory of South African history, always present, never resolved. *Cry, the Beloved Country*'s subtitle is *A Story of Comfort in Desolation*. This may be, but it is difficult to get past what invariably seems so intractable in our past: the oppression of black South Africans and their dispossession, forcing them into the meat grinders that are the mines; the wanton destruction of a beautiful land by those too poor to care about tomorrow; the all-too-common alienation between tribes, generations and people, the sadness, the pain.

Written nearly 70 years ago, much that is secondary in the novel – the ubiquitous crime, the populist demagoguery, the way the poor shuttle between apathy and anger – is still with us today. In a sense, this was confirmed by our walk, where neither the use of the land nor the status of those living upon it had changed that much. Cobbled together pondoks still lined the track, car tyres on tin roofs; curious, under-clothed children, snotty as they ran after us, issued giggles and shy hellos. The rural poor still walked the gravel roads that spun through the hills, spending long hours waiting in the sun for the inter-town taxis and, although they were now their own bosses, black workers still felled the forests. This, perhaps, was the deeper more generalised tragedy we glimpse so often in Paton's novel: the apparent timelessness of South African life and the multiple small tragedies of slow change or no change at all.

Yet this is also untrue. Pereira has mellowed since his barn-storming student days, learning to navigate along the some-times perilous tracks of everyday South African life with patience and care. Like a fair proportion of white people in the KwaZulu-Natal Midlands, he can *gooi die taal*. His Zulu is fluent and although he speaks it well, he uses it sparingly. The secret of getting much done with the current provincial power brokers, he told us candidly, was to always give the impression that your idea is someone else's. In this way, those more egotistical can bask in the light of success and adoration, while you slip into the background, never claiming responsibility but never having to take it either. And then there was always orange wine, made from trailer loads of stock discarded by others. Your wife thought the wine was only good for marinating pork but you understood its easy, deal-sealing properties far better.

As well as being socially adroit, Pereira is also an intensely practical man. He has corralled machinery, track, sheds and outbuildings from all over KwaZulu-Natal, buying it, taking it off people's hands and reassembling it in motley brilliance at Allwoodburn. With such endeavour, the siding is beginning to look like something proper and functioning, a small provincial station that sees its fair share of life, even if it no longer yields regular traffic. The 'Paton's Country Railway' sign hangs at the station entrance as you park your car and wander down to the platform, passing a bed of long-stemmed agapanthus as you go. Look further afield, across the golf course down in the valley, and you see the land Paton eulogised in the novel. A jacaranda or two is blushing mauve in the middle distance and the lands are rich green and resplendent, the lanes tree-lined, the air summer soft.

For all of his grubby practicality – Pereira's colleagues call him 'the hillbilly' – he is not without a streak of sentimentality. This manifests itself most obviously in his love of the novel. For him, it seems to function as the Bible might for others – a lodestar and guide for the perplexed. It is a book that has changed his life because it has animated the landscape spiritually and imaginatively, blessed it with words, thereby giving it a far richer existence than it might have had other-wise. Paton has literally sung the land into life for Pereira and, because of this, it has a resonance it would never have had before. Few pockets of South Africa are similarly ani-mated by fiction, pulled up and out of themselves by being given life in words. Perhaps J.M. Coetzee's road to De Doorns, along which Michael K pushes his wheelbarrow; maybe Marlene van Niekerk's Triomf or Dan Jacobson's Kimberley. The universe of Ixopo is now an unusually rich one, a home adorned with chapters and passages rather than kitchen units and dining-room chairs.

Pereira has tried to honour this and, as such, it makes him many things – a librarian, a cultural historian, a collector of that which might be forgotten and passed over. His great work has not been easy. Relationships between the other narrow-gauge enthusiasts and his lot aren't as convivial as you might expect. Last winter a veld fire, started in the scrub on the far boundary of the station, leapt a fence and burnt some of the wagons and rolling stock. Predictably, he has to deal with general obstruction, lack of money and the fact that he is reliant on the work of volunteers. All this considered, he retains an ability to charm money from the most Byzantine of government departments, the tightest of fists. We might even, in years to come, find ourselves humming along to tunes from *Cry, the Beloved Country – The Musical*.

* * *

The last leg of our journey took us past meadows dotted with cows so still they looked almost ornamental. Now and then we might look down off the tracks to see a stagnant, slime-encrusted dam or up to see a crow or pair of them, vaguely menacing in their dropsy-like flight, always identifiable by their squawky, disapproving cries. As we clipped along the sleepers, sometimes balancing on the tracks, sometimes walking alongside, the cows continued grazing idly and idly grazing. They looked at us in that empty-eyed way that cows have, a lazy gaze devoid of even the slightest curiosity. At one point we stopped for a sip of water. We looked into the forest and tried to make out whether trees lopped off about a metre from the base had been cut or burned. Some seemed gnarled and malformed by fire, others more cleanly cut. Perhaps both were true? There had been fire here as well as a time of felling, we realised. We listened to the sough and soft striving of the wind in the leaves and continued on our contented way, our legs beginning to feel that they needed to be relieved. It was time for a cup of tea or a beer. The constant awkwardness of seldom being able to place your foot on even ground was collecting in our legs. For me, it was time to sit down with my notebook and start recording my thoughts, reflecting on where I had been.

On this final stretch we noticed the upper half of a gigantic cross, mounted on the cusp of a nearby hill overlooking Ixopo. We were meandering with the tracks and so found that it moved, first to our right, then our left. After about 10 minutes we finally left it behind, negotiating our way past the broken bottles, plastic and litter strewn on the banks of the track. We walked behind the back of the local high school and past houses, cabins and occasional caravans. Soon we clipped into

CHAPTER 1 – Mountain View, via Orange Grove, to the Modderfontein Dynamite Factory

Top Left: The plunge along 9th Avenue, down past the Orange Grove plane trees.

Top Right: Sydenham Park: Albert Kimmerling piloted his Voisin biplane on Joburg's first recorded flight round about here.

CHAPTER 2 – Salem to Southwell

Bottom: The fat lemon trees of Southwell, in the gardens of the Church of St James.

CHAPTER 3 – Ramble on the farm Eildon – Baviaans River Valley
Top: Bitter Karoo: the lush heather of the Baviaans River.
Bottom: Pringle's *witgat:* poet Thomas Pringle composed some of the first verse written in English in South Africa under this very tree.

CHAPTER 4 – Carisbrooke via Stainton to Ixopo, Alan Paton country
Top: End of the line: the view through the cab of a disused steam engine, Ixopo, KwaZulu-Natal.
Bottom: The narrow-gauge railway from Carisbrooke to Ixopo is the line travelled by Rev. Stephen Kumalo in Alan Paton's *Cry, the Beloved Country.*

Left: Julian Pereira, the guiding force behind the narrow-gauge Paton's Country Railway in rural KwaZulu-Natal.
Bottom: Paton's Country Railway: end of the narrow-gauge line from Carisbrooke and Stainton.

CHAPTER 5 – Muizenberg station to Simon's Town
Top: The view from Dido Valley Cemetery, overlooking False Bay.
Bottom: Champion tree: the Monterey cypress at the entrance to the Dido Valley Cemetery, near Simon's Town.

CHAPTER 6 – Mooki St, Orlando, to Credo Mutwa Centre and the Oppenheimer Tower

Top: Credo Mutwa had a visionary and highly eccentric worldview: here is his Soweto garden of monsters, spirit ancestors and rondavels.
Bottom: Looming through the trees, Soweto's cinderblock structure, the Oppenheimer Tower.

CHAPTER 7 – Makapanstad ramble with Philip Kgosana

Top: The Lutheran church in Makapanstad. Philip Kgosana's father, a carpenter, helped carve the stairwell to the pulpit.

Bottom: As a 23-year-old, Kgosana led a march of 30 000 protesters to the Roeland Street Police Station, Cape Town. Here he stands, now 79, in the Lutheran Cemetery in Makapanstad, the hamlet in which he was born and grew up.

Top: Where 'Kortbroek' Kgosana first wore shorts, growing up in the family home, Makapanstad.

Bottom: Hardly used any more: the dusty old building in which Philip's father used to give his Sunday morning-sermons.

CHAPTER 8 – Kloof Nek to Kasteelpoort cableway via the Overseer's Cottage

Top: The Overseer's Cottage, passed during the early stages of the Table Mountain walk.

Bottom: The back of the De Villiers Dam wall (note the house-like features at the wall's base).

Top: The colour of orange: the tannin-stained water of the Table Mountain dams.

Bottom: The De Villiers Dam – one of Table Mountain's five reservoirs (note the low water level due to lack of rain).

CHAPTER 9 – Eikeboom in the Cederberg to the tableland up above

Top: A proud dad (middle) with sons, Sam (green T-shirt) and Jake (turquoise T-shirt) – walking in the Cederberg.

Bottom: Sam and Skye (a girl worth making alfresco tiramisu for).

Top: View from the top of the Sederhoutkloof, with Eikeboom about three kilometres back at the foot of the valley.

Bottom: The wild blue yonder: one of the Cederberg's fine sandstone roads.

CHAPTER 10 – The Tara Rokpa Centre ramble, Marico country

Top: A hand-carved headstone in the Oberholzer family graveyard, Groot Marico.

Bottom: The clear waters of the Marico Eye, with water lilies.

CHAPTER 11 – Following Gandhi's footsteps from Museum
Africa to the Hindu Crematorium

Top: View through the jacaranda shadow: Brixton Cemetery,
end point of the Gandhi walk.

Bottom: Hindu plaques at the Hindu Crematorium, Brixton Cemetery, Johannesburg.

Opposite Top: The Hindu Crematorium, Brixton, Johannesburg:
Gandhi campaigned for the crematorium, which was designed
by Hermann Kallenbach. Note the fluted red-brick chimneys
behind the two palm trees on the extreme right. This was the
original crematorium.

Opposite Bottom: The Hindu dead: these strangely beautiful plaques
are nailed to the base of gum trees in the cemetery.

CHAPTER 12 –
Voortrekker
Monument to
Freedom Park via
'Reconciliation
Road'
Left: The long walk
to reconciliation:
Freedom Day
walk at the foot
of the Voortrekker
Monument.

Right: Carling
Black Label
brigade: Vuka
Tshabalala (centre)
in Orlando Pirates
tracksuit, with
the peerless
Bangomuzi
Manyana (green
Nedbank Cup hat)
in the foreground.

Left: We salute
you: Freedom
Day at Freedom
Park (after
boerie rolls and
chakalaka).

Allwoodburn siding and its fabulous collection of rusted machinery. We had walked a small part of the Reverend Stephen Kumalo's long journey. As much as it's a journey starting in a crowded third-class carriage, the novel is also about a voyage of Kumalo's soul. A soul finally accorded a measure of comfort in desolation.

* * *

The next day, we caught a ride on the Paton train with about 70 or 80 others. Pulled by one of the orange General Electric locomotives, it hauled five or six carriages of various age and design full of joyful people. There were families and railway enthusiasts, children fizzing with expectation, adults with cellphone cameras and tablets working their way through every available angle and view. We joined a group of keep-your-own-counsel hillbillies, who nodded their heads slightly in muted greeting. One of them had a face disfigured in some terrible accident, another a long ponytail that stretched almost into the small of his back. He seemed dressed for combat. We smiled, tried not to stare and tiptoed as far away as possible. The train driver, we'd noticed earlier, was an Indian. His sleek Ford was parked on the siding and he was dressed with a certain jump, velveteen elbow patches to his jersey and a sharp point to his shiny shoes. His wife and teenage daughter were selling samoosas out of a giant Tupperware inside the station building and once everyone had boarded, he eased us away from the platform with a magnificent low growl, yanking on the chain above his head in the driver's cabin to signal we were on our way. We punted slowly down the line, admiring the scenery and feeling even the most gradual incline of the track. The hillbillies drank a seemingly inexhaustible supply of beer from a cooler box covered with black masking tape. The man with the reconstructed face actively sought out shadows and corners, scared to look at you for what he would see in your eyes. For a moment – just a moment – it became a line of plaintive sorrows. I felt pity for the man, his absence of a nose and the terrible scarring around his eyes, his face a smooth quilt of grafted skin from other parts of his body. Then I went back to being a little boy, sharing happy kisses with Lisa. We looked out of the carriage window, cheeks touching, watching great forests of wattle flow by.

5

FEAR AND LOATHING ON THE FISH HOEK BOARDWALK

Muizenberg via Kalk Bay, Fish Hoek and
Glencairn to Simon's Town — about 12 kilometres

What better place to start a False Bay walk than Mui-zenberg station, east-facing to greet the morning sun. It was the week before Christmas, normally a time of umbrellas and ice cream, a collection of shells for the Joburg windowsill, but now there was a cold offshore rip threatening the nation's time on the beach. Eight days before, our pathologically flaky president had dismissed Nhlanhla Nene, the Minister of Finance, replacing him with David (Des) van Rooyen, a serial underachiever and *agterschlepper*. A weekend of high drama followed the Van Rooyen announcement, with members of the banking community impressing upon Zuma that the decision was fatally lacking in both local and international appeal. On Sunday night the country heard that Van Rooyen had been shovelled sideways and Pravin Gordhan, Nene's predecessor, had been appointed in his place. While the rand tumbled to fresh lows amid the indecision, my family and I imagined we could hear a countrywide surge of relief. We breathed a sigh of one ourselves.

If relief was a companion that day, so, too, was gratitude, and trepidation and fear of the future. Such feelings were soon salved by the balm of everyday life, as the world around me awoke and went about its business. There was comfort to be gained from greeting joggers pounding down the boardwalk between Muizenberg and St James, slipping past svelte conversationalists in sarongs and droopy-brimmed hats as they made for the popular tidal pool and bathing houses at St James. At the beginning of the walk I had grabbed half a mussel shell off the beds on the rocks just north of Rhodes Cottage. As I walked, I rubbed it with my thumb, bringing out its lustre. It calmed me. Every so often I looked at its colours: a border of creamy purple fading to milky mauve and white at its centre. The half shell was to keep me company as I walked, a talisman and lucky charm. It reminded me of the casual bounty of the natural world, things I sensed but couldn't name. With the shell in my pocket, South Africa would be fine.

Continuing as the boardwalk edged out of Muizenberg, the morning rose in Christmas-holiday splendour, no wind, the sun climbing. I passed a *bergie* car guard who had slept rough in a narrow park on the seaward side of St James. All his worldly possessions seemed contained in a Jet plastic bag. He was doing his morning ablutions, wringing out his luminous car guard's vest under the park tap before drying it out and putting in on. I skipped past a group of what I took to be English tourists, legs milk-white in absurdly short skirts, and a trickle of locals coming out of the Kalk Bay Community Centre, rolled yoga mats under their arms. Just beyond the entrance to the Cape to Cuba café, a chef or waiter was sitting in the shade of an overhanging tree, calmly rolling a home-made cigarette or joint. Starlets were sitting in the pavement cafés, genuflecting before their new-generation iPhones. A boy, his hair expertly cut and gelled, sailed past on a skate-board. Traffic milled and stalled; folk sipped cappuccinos in the window of the Olympia Café and a man strolled down the street playing Christmas carols out of a battered saxo-phone. The Kalk Bay harbour was filled with slow rhythm, the seals in the corner, smelly and bored, twirling through their early-day routines like Berlin decadents. Already families were gathering in the shade of the viaduct, which carries the train line down to Fish Hoek, jabbering, laying down their picnic blankets and making themselves comfortable.

On the brick walkway close to the entrance to the Kalk Bay harbour is a granite milestone, with the number '17' etched in Roman numerals on its face. Erected by the Kalk Bay Historical Association, it refers to the original milestones, once planted at mile-long intervals between the Town House, off Greenmarket Square, and Simon's Town. Placed on the orders of Lord Charles Somerset, the milestones, laid between 1814 and 1815, served a dual purpose. They were, firstly, markers of distance for an expanding roadworks programme, but also served as a means to determine fares if you were travelling by cart or trap. In all likelihood, the original mile-stones were quarried from Robben Island, possibly by pris-oners awaiting a berth on a ship to Australia. The '17' dis-played on the front of the recently designed commemorative stone marks distance, and, give or take a few feet, it is 17 miles from Kalk Bay to Greenmarket Square. Appropriately, the commemorative milestone is placed close to where old photographs show the far smaller original once stood.

The railway came later, and by 1864 the line linked Cape Town's mainline station with Muizenberg via Wynberg, with trains between the two being known as 'Muizenberg Flyers' because there were no further stops on the route, enabling engines to hurtle down the line to Muizenberg at full throttle. By 1883 more progress had been made and the Muizenberg terminus was joined with St James and Kalk Bay. It took a full seven years after that, however, for the line to reach Simon's Town. The Kalk Bay harbour viaduct was built because the authorities wanted to avoid the track creating a barrier to the beach, thereby separating the place where the fishermen traditionally stowed their boats from the rest of the harbour. The viaduct was painstaking work and costly, as were the turns just out of Kalk Bay and the gentle glide down to the beach at Fish Hoek. The final extensions to the naval base at Simon's Town went at least three times over budget.

After passing the entrance to the harbour, noticing the gracious wooden hull of an old trawler in dry dock being scraped and repainted, I walked down the slow decline to Fish Hoek. The road here was being dug up for repairs, and although the workers had gone home for Christmas recess, their material – concrete blocks and paving stones – was everywhere. I walked carefully, crossing the road several times, avoiding bumper-to-bumper traffic as I passed Wooley's Tidal Pool down beneath me. Slightly beyond that were the remains of Clovelly Station. Now a bomb site of collapsed concrete, rusted jousts and mismatched walls, the station must have been an indulgence even in its heyday. It can't have been well patronised because the distance between Kalk Bay and Fish Hoek is short and serves too limited a population. Still, on previous holidays in the Cape, I found myself wondering what it was like to catch a train in such breathtakingly beautiful circumstances, sort of like watching an engine sail sleepily out of a children's bedtime story. Clearly, the authorities weren't quite as taken with the station's romance. Clovelly was closed down in 1990, with the Fish Hoek municipality and Metrorail arguing about who owned what and what their responsibilities were. Apparently, the municipality closed an underpass to the station, arguing it was unsafe, thereby blocking off one of the main access routes between it and the north-western side of Fish Hoek beach. The station had always balanced uneasily; with the sea hurling itself into the rocks below, and running repairs were a constant necessity and the closure of the underpass gave Metrorail the excuse they needed to finally close the station down. Now it wasn't a station but the location – I noticed, as I walked – for a long and doubtless necessary retaining wall.

One of the joys of walking is that it gives you time to see things you would otherwise miss. Walking Fish Hoek beach, shoes off, I saw and felt the following: 1) the lap of sea and sand on the soles of my feet; 2) a mini-cricket game with young parents and children, a dad exhorting his slightly cornered daughter to 'watch the ball' as she tried with difficulty to wield the bat; 3) municipal workers harvesting

103

massive strands of kelp from the beach and dragging them away; 4) a brisk morning walker in a pink long-sleeved top, passing me at least once (possibly twice) before I lazed my way to the boardwalk; 5) a group of young black bathers in the middle of the beach, gingerly approaching the small waves as they tried to keep their hair dry, their only company what appeared to be a white granny with her yet-to-learn-how-to-swim granddaughter; 6) the beach shark net, suspended at an acute diagonal from the rocks to a small section of the beach directly opposite the restaurant; 7) a group of what I took to be Vaalies (it was the accents that finally clinched it) setting out their stall for the day; the young men already had boeps, which their T-shirts failed by some measure to contain. Although I will say this: they were extremely well prepared food-wise; 8) the colour of the water (difficult to describe with complete fidelity), ranging from blue-black in the kelp-heavy colder waters to turquoise and ultramarine closer to shore; 9) Clovelly station (or the remains of it) rusting behind me like some battleground relic; 10) the charming peacefulness of the scene, aided by the benign Fish Hoek waves, good for the young, the infirm and the first-time bather; best of all, though, was 11) – the young woman with her dog on the boardwalk, standing next to the miniature lighthouse with horizontal yellow-and-white stripes. Wearing a hat and polka-dot shorts, and holding a small, tousle-haired dog out in front of her, she was laughing as she waited to be photographed by her mother or an elderly relative. Sun-splashed, almost giddy, excited with all of her being, this was the best day of her life; finally, 12) – the description of a walk along the beach wouldn't be complete without mentioning the important search for sand of the requisite firmness, neither too soft nor too wet. It is a firmness that claims the pad of one's foot perfectly, without collapsing like dune sand or sinking away like sand in deeper water. Try as I might, my quest for the perfect stretch of sand was in vain. There was enough to see, besides; enough to keep the sketchbook of my mind busy, enough to keep me buoyant, sun-blessed, sweaty and alive.

After padding along the boardwalk in bare feet, I found a free bench in partial shade. I peeled a banana, rummaged around in my daypack for pens and notebook, and adjusted my cap, sipping from my bottle of water. I'd passed a group of oldies, resting themselves on the brightly painted stone benches like some long-lost aristocracy, and men with closed eyes, shirts off, soaking up the sun. There were walkers and hand-holders, the flow of low tones and quiet ease. All around, the sea went about its amiable lolling, kelp heaving and snorting between the boulders. I'd passed talkers, occasional readers, worshippers of light. The air was still and gnawingly hot as I rearranged my legs to find just a little more shade. I scribbled some impressions, tried to brush most of the beach sand from my feet and put on my much-travelled Timberlands. I had some way to go, my next section a battle with the nothing-to-see drudgeries of the route out of Fish Hoek towards Glencairn, what I expected to be the most uninspiring section of the morning's walk. Soon up, I pottered past the boulders and stone pines, so stately they seemed eternal. I crossed the railway line over the pedestrian bridge as I began the long curve toward the cove of Glencairn.

It turned out that I was wrong about this stretch's lack of charm. The views here were good, the road wide, making it almost possible to forget the steady drift of passing traffic. As I clipped along the generous pavement, I noticed rocks down to my left on the False Bay side, and regular clumps of dark-green bush spilling over the wall separating the pavement from them and sea. Some of the bushes had been moulded to form little *hoekies* or sleeping holes and they smelled. Discarded clothes and clapboard and litter were strewn where the homeless had spent the night, the reek of piss and sweat and shit mingling with the tang of rotting kelp. I ploughed on, instinctively recoiling from what I saw. It was that familiar South African compound: distaste, hopelessness, pity, that oddly familiar sensation you could almost watch creep across your skin. I walked through my disgust, wondering vaguely who had been there last and where they were now, and how they managed. Did such natural beauty make their wandering lives better or worse? For them, such abundance was surely an irrelevance. They were still exposed, still hungry, still desperate; the casual dance of the sun on the sea not something they saw – or thought about. In other respects, the poor are more observant than we care to admit. They know where to find protection for the night, shelter from the wind, water. As I walked towards Glencairn beach I noticed that this line of coast provided the wandering homeless with more chances for a thin existence than perhaps I realised. At Glencairn there were nooks and crannies adjacent to a storm-water drain. You could burrow onto or behind an old bench, or find meagre comfort behind the odd outbuilding or ablution block. There were opportunities to camp for the night, make a brew, boil yourself a pot of mussels over a driftwood fire. In the silence of early morning you could wash in one of the many derelict tidal pools, and hang your clothes on the rocks to dry, watching the first light creep over the bluffs on the far side of the bay.

Of all I discovered on this walk, these tidal pools – remote, lonely, charming – gave me the most pleasure. On either side of Glencairn beach, several of them were fronted by peeling danger signs warning bathers of the pitfalls of swimming or paddling. On closer inspection, this was just the council being careful. The pools were almost perfectly intact, but for a partial crumbling here or a more substantial break in the defences there. Alongside one pool I passed, I noticed a pup tent on the beach, and an *oupa* lolling in the shallows like a bath-time duck, his grandchildren frolicking nearby. As I passed, I saw that the pools were often mirror-still, full of the clearest water. You could sit in them and see to the bottom, or swim or paddle about, searching for shrimp or the occasional trapped fish. If paddling was too energetic, you could simply cup sea sand in your hands and watch it disperse, wondering pleasantly what your dredging might find. I should have stopped my walk at this point and had a swim but didn't want to intrude. Although they are pub-lic places, I somehow felt that the serenity of these pools would be jealously guarded, those within them ill-disposed to sharing.

If a dictionary were ever compiled on the vernacular items and architecture of everyday South African life – 'B' for block-houses, 'C' for Cape Dutch gables, 'W' for windmills – 'T' would surely contain an entry for tidal pools. They are our great egalitarian blessing – free and open to all. There were far more tidal pools on this stretch of coast than I'd imagined before walking it, and far more on the False Bay coast – little gems, tucked away, sparkling in neat obscurity. I remember once holidaying at Gordon's Bay, when our three sons were still dwarfed by their beach towels, meandering down the coast to Rooi Els one late-December afternoon. Close to the Kogel Bay holiday resort, we discovered a massive tidal pool and, on a whim, decided to stop. We spent an afternoon there with hundreds of locals, families from Gordon's Bay and the Strand, jumping, swimming and shouting – one of the most purely relaxing three or four hours of my life. The pool was big enough to hold almost everyone, with a beach for the overspill off to one side. It was in good upkeep and clean. We threw a tennis ball to each other over bobbing heads and dived and bombed and splashed. When we were tired Lisa and I covered our shoulders with towels to protect us from the falling sun and watched, touching toes underwater as they were nibbled by swarms of sand-coloured fish. People are rendered playful by water. Time slows down and, as it does, you can bask in watery splendour together. It was a place, I remember thinking to myself at the time, where we could all be South Africans. Petty apartheid took insidious forms, but, for me, the most neurotic expression of the philosophy was the idea that people of different races couldn't share the same water.

Glencairn itself was sparsely populated, a couple of families, some couples, the nearby road possibly running too close for privacy and comfort. Still, you get no beaches whatsoever on the Highveld, so we tend not to be as discerning as the locals. To us, the wastes of Noordhoek seem like a glimpse of heaven, and even Glencairn – let's slot it in as a B-category beach experience – seemed quaint enough to savour. Such feelings were sharpened when I saw a dad and his toddler on a surfboard. As the board bowed toward shore, he lifted her to her feet and they bobbled on the dying wave until the board snagged on the sand. I thought it expert – almost worthy of a circus trick – and marvelled at how practised they seemed. I've thought about it since. It was almost pre-verbal: sensations and colours, no words, happening in a realm before language. It happened before tension, before disappointment, before sibling rivalry and favourites. A perfect moment – a perfect wave – before life and doubt crowd in.

Throwing off my beachy reveries, I headed to the Dido Valley Cemetery, on the other side of the main road. The cemetery climbs a gentle hill and has three entrances guarded by heavy wooden gates, all three open to varying degrees. The one through which I passed was partly blocked by a Monterey cypress. Once upright, the tug of the northeaster had slowly toppled it off the vertical, and now it acted as a green arch over the entrance itself, propped up by an over-burdened pole. It was, said the nearby plaque, erected by the Simon's Town Historical Society, 'a champion tree'. I liked the tree and stood in its shadow but thought wryly, while trying to savour its smell and the sweep of its branches, that this was rather stretching the bounds of the public's credulity.

It might have been a champion tree but now it looked rather as if it was out for the count in the bottom of the seventh, dignified but falling, and soon to hit the floor.

Each denomination in the cemetery had its parcel of land, with sections in the graveyard's upper reaches also reserved for paupers and the stillborn. Dead Jews couldn't rub bones with dead Mohammedans; dead Methodists weren't to stray in death onto ground reserved for those who had worshipped in the Dutch Reformed Church when alive. I wandered about, noticing the gravestones and collapsed graves, the creep of the beach sand in which they were placed, memorial stones bumping sleepily into each other as everywhere the ground shifted and subsided. Although the main road traffic wasn't far away, it was lonely in here, more so because the rigour of demarcation was being slowly undone. Beneath the bright-blue sky, the sun sharp as it shrivelled the dune grass and gnawed at the blighted shrubs, bones were rubbing together in the grand democracy of death. Beneath my feet, the rigid demarcations were collapsing. Despite the best intentions of the authorities to keep the cemetery alive, it had – in a manner of speaking – reached its final resting place.

It was, in all respects, a dead end.

Towards the end of my ramble, I noticed what appeared to be the best-kept section of the cemetery – on the Simon's Town side. It was maintained by the SANDF and was separated from the rest of the graveyard by a road. This section contained the graves of all those sailors and officers who had lost their lives in the course of duty at the Simon's Town naval base, whether South African, British, Russian or French.

I wondered – or tried to wonder – about what I saw, as the gardener greeted me and went about trimming the lawn and freshening the beds. Who was John Postlethwaite, for instance, the HMS *Carlisle*'s leading stoker? He was 26 when he lost his life on 1 March 1935. His gravestone was not erected by the navy, which he had served, but by subscriptions from shipmates long forgotten. Then there was the matelot of the French navy, Sebastien Nedelec, who had died six years later, in the early years of the war. What of their stories? Their lives? It is strange to think that there is someone in France who might be related to Sebastien or know of him, who might one day start excavations and ask questions – who might even board the train and get off at Simon's Town before walking back towards Glencairn for a wreath-laying visit.

During my walk I hadn't seen trains in either direction on the route between Fish Hoek and Simon's Town. Clearly, the lines' early travails set a distinguished precedent because on the long, flat sweep into Simon's Town proper I passed three or four Metrorail trucks. They were repairing the line with a giant gizmo, part can-opener, part clamp. The trucks were parked partially in the road and I hurried to pass them with traffic roaring past, so I wasn't as observant as perhaps I should have been. All I remember was a stressed foreman, kneeling down on the tracks as he pondered his next move. My next one was to walk on the tracks towards Long Beach, hurdling them and then negotiating the fists and knuckles of rocks as I found the comfort of beach sand and again took off my shoes. The beach was sparsely peopled. A diving lesson was taking place for first-time divers at the far end, while, closer by, two stocky, freshly painted rowboats with racy red-and-green stripes pulled clear of the high-water mark.

As I walked, I noticed two tarpaulins suspended from poles to provide a makeshift shelter over the beach. There was a community of 15 or 20 relaxing in the shadows, their wash basins and cooking implements and bedding cast around. Children from the group surfed in the shallows as I passed them, part friendly, part bored, the spool of lazy curiosity in their eyes. Just who was this *oupa* with shoes in his hands, a daypack on his back? Further along, I noticed the scuba divers, black heads and goggles protruding from the benign water like frogs with sea-bottom jewels. I only had a little way to go before spending the rest of the morning in the offices of the Simon's Town Historical Society nearby, flicking through files and maps of the cemetery. I had pretty much walked my road. It was the end of the line.

* * *

After seven years of rock-breaking toil, flattening the track bed and confronting winter wash-aways, the line from Kalk Bay finally broke through to Simon's Town in 1890. The official opening was a splendid one, an occasion for speeches and a feast in a nearby meadow. A military band played 'God Save the King'. 'Every ship, building, wall, fence and pole was smothered in bunting, decorations and flowers,' according to Catherine Knox and Cora Coetzee in their book *Victorian Life at the Cape 1870–1900*. 'A triumphal arch of "rustic beauty" was erected over the main street. Flags fluttered against the sky. Shopkeepers had entered into informal competition with one another in line of imaginative displays. Turner's Drapery sported a pink banner expressing "Welcome to the Iron Horse" in large blue letters and, just for good measure, a miniature railway set was arranged in front of this. The station was opened by Cecil John Rhodes, who was accompanied by the treasurer, John X. Merriman, the attorney-general, James Rose Innes, the general manager of the Cape Government Railways, Charles Elliott, and a host of other important personages.'

There was more. That afternoon, after a lull in the formalities, the owners of the line, the Cape Government Railways, allowed for a free ride to Kalk Bay and back for all comers. Regardless of age, colour or class, everyone would be accommodated. The carriages were crammed and off they went, steaming slowly down the line I had in part just walked, past Long Beach, around Glencairn and towards Fish Hoek, and up the final gentle slope through Clovelly towards Kalk Bay. I find it joyous to imagine the bliss of that December afternoon back in 1890, the waddling train with children spilling out of the windows, the shrieks of delight and the never-before-seen views.

'Looked at from this perspective it almost looks as if the train is balancing on the sea.'

The free ride on the train wasn't only an occasion to be stored in the cobwebby vaults of memory; it was also a grand day for imperial capital. Academics remind us that with the coming of the railways in England came the standardisation of time. 'In 1847, British train companies put their heads together and agreed that henceforth that all train timetables would be calibrated to Greenwich Observatory time, rather than the local times of Liverpool, Manchester or Glasgow,' writes Yuval Noah Harari in *Sapiens: A Brief History of Humankind*. 'More and more institutions followed the lead of the train companies. Finally, in 1880, the British government took the unprecedented step of legislating that all timetables in Britain must follow Greenwich. For the first time in history, a country adopted a national time and obliged its population to live according to an artificial clock rather than local ones of sunrise-to-sunset cycles.'

It would be interesting to know if the same thing happened in South Africa, and whether regional time collapsed into a standardised national time with the tentacle-like thrust of the railways. Whether what happened in Britain came to pass in South Africa or not, the walk was remarkable for offering a glimpse into the everyday workings of imperialism. The idea was to overcome the tyranny of distance by integrating Simon's Town into Cape Town as completely as possible. Pathways and cart tracks were formalised and turned into roads; milestones marked and measured the roads, allowing for prices for goods and services to be fixed in a way everyone could understand. At the end of the road from Muizenberg, just as travellers and services were entering Simon's Town proper, there used to be a gate and toll house, and there's a small memorial plaque on the site today. The gate and toll house lasted for about 85 years – from roughly 1815 to the turn of the century – and would to some extent have been eclipsed by the bustle and busy thrum of the railways. In 1990, the 100th anniversary of the line's arrival, a memorial train ride departed from Cape Town station and found its way to Simon's Town. The occasion was lavish and widely celebrated. Brochures and descriptions are filed away in the drawers of the Simon's Town Historical Society's offices. After my walk I paged through the brochures and looked at the photographs, and wondered why 25 years ago seemed like a political and social eternity away. Nowadays the train to Simon's Town seems less a public service than a piece of charming moving scenery. You realise when walking that the passenger train is a functioning relic. Its purpose nowadays is more cosmetic than practical, a reminder of what was rather than what might be. On this stretch of coast it's as much a feature of the picture postcard as the St James bathing houses and the Kalk Bay minstrel and his crumpled sax.

After my walk and time in the library I settled down to read the previous day's papers, all of their columnists keen to rake through the weekend's still-hot coals. In *Business Day*, Anton Harber argued that JZ's decision to boot Nene was significant because it told us important things not only about the president's personality, but also about the peculiar churnings of South African democracy. 'It quickly became clear that the announcement was even more shockingly arbitrary as Zuma had not consulted his own Cabinet, party or allies. This from a president who has frequently extolled the importance of collective decision-making and responsibility,' wrote Harber.

In the same newspaper, Steven Friedman took a different

tack, arguing that he was saddened by the reaction to the Gordhan reappointment and all that preceded it, in that he believed such comment mistakenly represented a victory as a defeat. He went on to say that reinstalling Gordhan was a slap in the face for Zuma's rural power base, the patronage politicians who want to get their hands on Treasury purse strings. 'All this signals to anyone who tries to cross the line by turning the Treasury into their fiefdom is that they will be pushed back by the markets, political opponents and urban citizens. It is unlikely anyone will try a repeat soon. This must be a huge plus for those who do not want public institutions to be captured for private gain. It shows that the system works – so well that it has defeated the predators in less than a week.'

Best of all was Rian Malan's *Daily Maverick* post, his *breker* journalism thundering along at breakneck speed. He argued for tax revolt, and the creation of an alternative 'Mzanzi tax', which would be used to buy mielie-meal to feed the poor. As with all Malan's journalism, it was not only the content of his argument but the quality of the voice that held one. It was engaged and contemptuous of *handlangers*, and had that blowing-in-the-wind rawness you'd come to expect. You could look through the words, beyond the page and into the waters of Malan's tortured *joller* soul. It was like being in therapy together.

I remember reading excerpts of Malan's *My Traitor's Heart* anthologised in *The New Yorker* all those years ago. A friend had torn the book extracts out of someone else's magazine and we circulated them among ourselves in a frenzy of admiration and furtive delight. I had never read about Johannesburg suburban life – reggae, zol, avoiding the army, the pure unadulterated weirdness of parents – in this way before and we embraced him as one of our own. We couldn't help but compare Malan with Nadine Gordimer, who at about this time was interviewed in *Vanity Fair*. She described white South Africans as being members of an extended country club, which enraged us, while allowing herself to be photographed in immaculately pressed khaki like some sort of local Karen Blixen. Gordimer seemed hopelessly self-regarding and snotty, while Malan had front-line authenticity. Behind that was something even more fascinating – a kind of clanging vulnerability. His writing seemed artless because of it, although, of course, it was gelled and highly styled, so you needed to be aware of how well groomed his lurid African horror stories were for American consumption.

By the time the book eventually came out, I was living in London, having fled yet another call-up to an infantry battalion in Oudtshoorn, scraping a living as an undertrained teacher in a soulless south London comprehensive. When I wasn't on public transport ('we regret to inform you that this service will terminate at Victoria'), I was often doing no more than trying to get my classes to sit still. Sometimes I succeeded, and felt I was getting somewhere, reaching some part of their head that hadn't yet been touched. On others I clung on grimly while pandemonium reigned and feisty Nigerians called Yetunde casually tossed chairs out of the first-floor window. I spent much of my time on buses or tubes, so I bought a reduced hardback copy of the original American edition – mountains of the book were everywhere in London in 1990 – and ravaged it as I crossed the Thames on my journeys south. My friends and I couldn't stop talking about it for weeks. I remember seances – a very Malan word – on the floors of under-furnished basement flats in Notting Hill Gate and arguments, sometimes heated, about his politics and worldview. Despite the disagreements, we secretly, and not-so-secretly, loved the book. It was about us, our warped country and sometimes schizophrenic state of mind. We knew about the Augie de Kokers and Betty Goods of this world; we were all familiar with Dennis Moshweshwe, 'the polished swell'. These folk were part of our inheritance and psychic landscape. Our identification was absolute and, I think now, probably a little facile. Not that you would have convinced us of this at the time, for we were all hopelessly homesick. During my five-year period away, I probably read more South African fiction and listened to more kwela and borrowed accordion jive than I ever had or have done since. I consumed *The Guardian* and the *Independent*, in which David Beresford and John Carlin reported from Johannesburg daily. I wrote fat, terrifyingly embarrassing letters home to my parents in Highlands North (my mum always stressed the 'extension', as did I). Looking back on it all, I realise I was in no more than a prolonged holding pattern, arcing in a slow descent home.

Reading anything by Malan now and you can't help notice its period flavour, his heart-achingly poignant use of words like 'jol', 'braai', *'vrot'* and 'dude'. He knows this; he knows we know this, and it makes for collusion and shared sadness.

Malan has become like the very things he described himself hankering after when he lived in LA writing music reviews under the nom de plume 'Nelson Mandela'. He pined for the Highveld light. He remembered Mrs Ball's chutney and thick wedges of Wicks chewing gum. He watched baggage handlers go about their work after jetting in from the States and burst into tears. He has become just another flavour of the sentimental times, an exclusive club which features much of what he describes in the book. There's Dollar Brand and bank bags full of 'Durban poison', Morrissey doing his androgynous, slightly loopy thing on the video to 'This Charming Man', James Phillips and friends pogo-ing into 'the lurch' at Jamesons on wild Friday nights. All of his subsequent work is coloured by the glow cast by *My Traitor's Heart* – both a blessing and a curse for someone who has never managed to slip the noose of his incredible early success.

Yet I'd be lying if I didn't admit there weren't – ahem – still a place in my heart for the book. Malan seemed to get it. He knew the limits of identification. He understood that a sizeable proportion of the white left were slumming it until it all became hot and uncomfortable, upon which they'd skedaddle for a sofa in Hampstead. He hammered a wedge into the crack between what you said and what you truly felt, and he carried on hammering until he had himself a little masterpiece. That his masterpiece has aged a little gracelessly might say something about how far we have come from the period he describes. It's a cheeky thought, one that doesn't quite square with the addictive pessimism of the times. You would think, reading the peacocks and professional chair sitters of the *Daily Maverick*, that corruption and patronage politics had strangled the life out of South Africa. It hasn't. And I know this because everywhere I walked people were going about the business – sometimes proud, sometimes hurried, sometimes hopelessly confused – of simply staying alive.

6
SOFASONKE CITY

Mooki St, Orlando, to the Oppenheimer Tower and Credo Mutwa Centre, Soweto, via Vilakazi St — about 10 kilometres

Soweto might have been called 'Sofasonke City'. It might also have been called 'Sputnik' or 'Oppenheimerville'. It could possibly have been called 'Coon's Kraal' or 'Vergenoeg' or 'Darkiesuburban', even 'Creamland'. In the end, however, none of these entries, submitted to a naming competition started by the Johannesburg City Council's Department of Non-European Affairs, took the judges' fancy. They decided to keep it safe and, in honouring South Africa's long-standing love of the literal, it was decided to call the township Soweto, an acronym for South-Western Townships. With such a dull name, they presumably reasoned, it wouldn't draw too much attention to itself. It could take its place alongside the plentiful supply of 'Vlakfonteins', 'Middelburgs' and 'Vaalwaters' without anyone really noticing. Here were names without flourish or poetry, as tangible as rocks in the veld. With ordinary names, they became ordinary places. When it came to Soweto, you knew exactly where you stood – and in more ways than one.

My guide through Soweto for the day was Vuka Gladstone Tshabalala. Vuka owned the self-proclaimed oldest house in Soweto, about which I had written a *Mail & Guardian* story, and although wary of his claims, I liked him. He was a goofy hustler with large, lively eyes who wore his replica Orlando Pirates jersey with great puffed-up pride. Most of all, I liked him for the little things. He maintained, for example, a small fleet of durable pronouns. In his text messages and mails he pushed them into reliable service, talking about 'we' and 'one', what 'we' had planned, and what 'one' was going to do about putting his Mooki Street house on the heritage map. It was a gambit of ownership, of propriety, and it conferred an importance on his projects that perhaps they didn't have. Vuka may have been afflicted by a mild case of hubris, but I didn't mind. He had chutzpah and cunning. I saw the operator within and smiled quietly in admiration.

Come to think of it, he reminded me a little of the Pringles of the Baviaans River. Like them, he was forging a tradition. They used Thomas Pringle, no more than a temporary sojourner on their land, really, to forward their claims, while Vuka used the memory of James 'Sofasonke' Mpanza to advance his. For Vuka, Mpanza represented the authentic spirit of Soweto, a quick-witted maverick who rallied a group of women frustrated by the council's *slapgat* approach to building houses and urged them to build their own. Mpanza lived and died in the backstreets of Orlando East nearby and Vuka was besotted with his demagoguery and womanising exuberance. Most of all, Mpanza had somehow escaped the clutches of the party, who were doing their best to sanitise

Soweto's history as a story of the ANC's political virtue. Vuka was having none of it. He saw Mpanza as a heretic and dangerous outlier. He would hitch his wagon to Mpanza's famous horse and ride for all he was worth.

Vuka's appropriation of the royal 'we' wasn't the only example of his being the official curator of Mpanza's memory. I arrived on a wet Saturday morning in January bearing gifts – purple grapes from our ageing vine. As Vuka's son went off to wash them, I stood outside his house with sundry old-timers in training gear and smart running shoes, slowly realising that Vuka had subtly hijacked the walk. In the planning phase I mentioned he could invite a few guests. 'The more the merrier,' I remember blithely texting. Now here I was, right in the middle of the first annual 'James Sofasonke Mpanza Memorial Big Walk'. An SABC camera-man videoed every step we took and Vuka asked us to write our names and contact details on a sheet in his black-backed file. I hadn't imagined such formality. I'd somehow thought of a walk as a looser, more freewheeling affair, but here we were, about to embark on an 'event'. It was the slickest piece of salesmanship I'd ever witnessed.

When everyone had finally gathered, we set off, leaving the Orlando Baptist church opposite Vuka's house and threading towards the Orlando Stadium in its Lafarge cement cladding. Rounding the stadium, we slipped down behind it, passing a scrap merchant (Mighty's Hardware) as we filled our lungs and started to enjoy being finally on the move. Mpanza was a complete footballer, according to Vuka, 'a middle-fielder, a defender and prolific goal scorer' all rolled into one. Born in 1889, he served a 13-year prison sentence for murdering an Indian trader when still relatively young and, after doing his time, arrived on the Rand, much as Absalom Kumalo had done in *Cry, the Beloved Country*.

Mpanza clearly had a talent for falling foul of authority because not long after arriving in Jozi he was expelled from Bertrams, a working-class suburb full of purpose-built houses east of Ellis Park. He moved to Soweto and in 1934 started the Orlando Boys' Club, a youth club housed in a draughty hall with a couple of dartboards. Although it was nothing special, such civic amenities were few and far between in the Soweto of the 1930s, and at the club you could join a dance group, form a band, or simply hang out. Three years later Mpanza took the logical next step for a football-mad community, and thus Orlando Pirates Football Club was born. 'When they sing Pirates' praises that's why they sing about the "Black Ones of James Mpanza",' Tshabalala told me proudly as we walked.

The south-western corner of Orlando Stadium is directly opposite the meander in the Klip River where Mpanza encouraged local women to erect makeshift shelters mixed with more permanent structures. The authorities weren't taking their applications for houses in the rapidly expanding suburb of Orlando seriously enough, he believed, and, losing patience, the women started building shacks and lean-tos. They were admirably industrious. They used hessian sacks and corrugated tin, and in some cases even managed to sink foundations into the ground. Turn off the nearby road today and cross the river, and you can still see traces and outlines of their dwellings. The land is crisscrossed with rubble, occasional twisted metal and deep-set concrete. Among the shacks must have been some well-built, more permanent structures. The outlines are still here, like dinosaur footprints, relics of what was. On my first visit, which had been in winter, I imagined sadness hanging just above my head, like mist. As the sun went down and the air settled just above the water of the river it must have been cold in these makeshift houses and shelters. What would it have been like with not enough warmth, not enough blankets, not quite enough food – a future as dark and impenetrable as night?

Mpanza's leadership and encouragement in all of this led to his sometime nickname 'Magebhula', meaning 'the one who grabbed land'. For all his jolly charm, he was an old-fashioned rural patriarch. I wonder how much real work he did. How many bricks did he bake or foundations did he sink? He was a physically small man and his stature was increased by trotting everywhere on his horse. I don't imagine he dismounted too often to muck in. He was above that, both literally and figuratively. The leader, the ideologue, the seer.

Given his political and social importance, I almost expected to see a statue of him somewhere – perhaps on horseback in the Orlando Stadium precinct, rearing for the sky. When I asked Vuka about it, he told me that this absence of official recognition was because Mpanza was too much of a populist firebrand. More importantly, he was never a member of the ANC, so he had quietly been written out of Soweto's official history. But such was his attractiveness that he would always bubble into the waters of the official narrative, making them less calm than many pretended, a geyser from the depths of popular memory. It wasn't the first time on my walks around the country that the living had appropriated the fancies of the dead for political gain. This is what popular history was all about, after all, an arm wrestle between competing versions of the past. I was reminded of Klement Gottwald and Vladimir Clementis, the Czech leaders written about by Milan Kundera in *The Book of Laughter and Forgetting*, and how their story is applicable not only to Czechoslovakia just after World War II, but how infinitely it might be extended. So much so, in fact, that it has taken on the shape of a political parable.

In 1948 the two politicians take to the podium to greet the people, Gottwald as the newly installed leader of the Communist Party, Clementis his beaten rival. It is a bitterly cold day and, in a gesture of profound magnanimity, Clementis takes off his fur hat and puts it on Gottwald's hatless head. Amid increasing state paranoia, Clementis, the man with the beautiful name, is executed four years later. The party propagandists breezily cut and paste him out of the official record. He is, in Kundera's perfect phrase, 'airbrushed out of history'. He doesn't appear in the official narrative and certainly doesn't appear in photos of the two on the podium on that cold day back in 1948. But the censors – perhaps forgetting – leave behind the hat. It is all that remains of Vladimir Clementis.

After inspecting what remained in the bend of the river, we crossed a main road and headed into suburban Soweto, stretching awake on a Saturday morning. Homeowners were out with their weeders and lawnmowers, trimming borders, cutting the grass. A group of youngsters had gathered for football practice in a park, taking shelter from the sun under a rickety wooden gazebo with a palm-frond roof. There was life on the street, the stately cruise of old Jettas, the quicker pace of recently bought Polos and buffed Figos and Sparks, with younger drivers behind the wheel. Most streets had a spaza shop or cubbyhole, out of which came a slow leak of items. I saw a man return home with a sachet of curry powder for dinner. A threesome of girls passed me, listening to a playlist on their cellphone through shared earplugs. Later I heard jazz tumbling merrily out of an invisible window. Everywhere the township was busying itself with errands and Saturday-morning chores. Washing, visits to the hairdresser, a quick natter with friends. Sometimes there was loitering and vague suspicion but for the most part people were either polite or uninterested. As I took all this in, I realised that it hadn't taken me long to find my way to the back of our walking group. I was often sidelined by taking notes or the fact that I can meander into a sort of *dwaal*. By the time I looked up from gazing at something or scribbling my illegible notes, the group had disappeared round the next bend.

Before long we found ourselves on Soweto's famous Vilakazi Street. There were stalls and concessions selling brightly coloured African shirts, T-shirts, Madiba memorabilia. I examined a blue plaque outside the main entrance of the Phefeni Junior Secondary School (active in the '76 riots) and noticed that Soweto's ubiquitous poplars were already changing colour, green fading to leaves of fragile pale yellow. A busload of what appeared to be German tourists was inching up the street, admiring the view from their luxury interior, and I took off my cap and bowed to the gallery amid much silent laughter. Soon I passed restaurants and shebeens, and a shop advertising itself as the Soweto Snake Show. According to their sign, they had anacondas, corn snakes, boa constrictors and what they called 'Berme pythons', which I guessed would be Burmese pythons. I liked the sign but was in no hurry to see the snakes. It was getting hot now, the heat sitting on us like a wet blanket, and I noticed that Simon Moloko, my struggling partner for the last while, had disappeared. I bumped into him later on, wondering how he'd managed to get in front of me, and he sheepishly owned up to having caught a ride in the SABC cameraman's car. Further along we noticed a group of five young beauty queens, long-legged and wrapped in rich red-and-white satins. They poked about on their stilt-like heels, black curls cascading onto their shoulders like grapes, gathering on the curb for selfies or cellphone photos, strangely oblivious to the world around them.

As I walked – Vuka was now long gone, leading operations from the front – I began to make sense of what I was seeing. The houses were generally smaller than what I was used to in suburban Johannesburg and stood on smaller plots of land. Although humble, most were well cared for and well tended. Placing big rocks between your front wall and the roadside seemed to be a theme – presumably to deter strangers from parking their cars outside your house. I noticed a general absence of burglar bars, electric fences and barbed wire. There were no rapid-response vehicles with private security personnel in paramilitary uniforms cruising the streets, no tin signs next to doorbells drawing attention to the owners' security company of choice. Street lights, although not everywhere, seemed to be in good condition. Sometimes the gantry-like 'Apollos', as they were called in the township, stood tall and their spooky yellow light would bathe the township at nightfall. Trees – planes, Chinese elms, pepper trees, poplars, the occasional shy cypress – were everywhere. Communal and ambiguous plots of vacant land were usually litter-strewn and the low-lying marshland near the Klip River often stinky, but private property was swept, polished, trimmed. Soweto had a strong sense of itself, a swaggering communality. There was a pride in this city of reeds and rebels, clamour and soul, that you will not find elsewhere.

As the walk continued beyond Vilakazi Street, the group became even more spread out, like a fully extended concertina. I was surprised at how many clinics and crèches there seemed to be. Dube Vocational appeared to be now occupied by the local Traffic Department. We passed SHAP Park, 'SHAP' being an acronym for the Self-Help Association of Paraplegics. Further along, in Mofolo Central, was the Rebone Botshelo Children's Centre, Day Care and Pre-School. Perhaps the schools and kindergartens were slightly underprovided, with not enough equipment or crayons or carers. But the face they showed the world suggested otherwise. Walls were freshly and neatly painted with the names of the institutions; playgrounds were swept and beds neatly tended. Here was a city with a reputation to uphold.

This impression was reinforced a little further along, when we passed through Mofolo Park in a gradual sweep towards the June 16 Memorial Acre. The trees in the park, planes mainly, had just been pruned, and a muddle of wood, branches and sawdust lined the pathway. I examined the care with which the pruners had gone about their business. The branches were cleanly cut and well shaped. Walking our dogs the next day in suburban Kensington, I noticed that the council had been doing exactly the same thing along Langermann Drive. Here, the old oaks had also been pruned, their bark stained black from the traffic fumes and Joburg's increasing grime. In Soweto the trees were younger. There was more sap in the limbs. In time, they would grow stately. Those who walked or drove through Mofolo Park would mark their lives by the size and colour of what they passed. In 50 years' time Soweto's trees will be as beautiful and loved as the trees of Johannesburg, like the chaotic cascade of oaks down Cyrildene Hill on Friedland Avenue. Or the tide of cork oaks that spreads from West Park Cemetery and Emmarentia in the west through Old Edwardians and the Virgin Active in Houghton all the way to Bezuidenhout Valley. I know of solitary cork oaks on the playing fields of Queens High. There are others at Huddle Park, close to the Modderfontein interchange, some of them magnificent, with peeling, almost fleshy bark and dark-green prickly leaves. After that they seem to diminish. As one heads east towards Edenvale and Germiston, they thin out, eventually disappearing. I wonder why? Did birds not fly in this direction? Did the prevailing winds simply blow elsewhere? Were the cork oaks prevented from their eastward sweep by the highways that began to necklace the city – the M2 and the R24 as they head off to the airport and Benoni? What is the mystery of the trees?

As we walked, I couldn't stop myself from picking up a chunk of freshly logged London plane. It was about eight inches thick and just fitted into the palm of my hand. I lugged it along on the rest of the journey as a kind of memento. I brought it home and stood it upright on the partition separating our kitchen and TV room, near the wine rack. It was a couple of days before I saw Lisa again. She was in Cape Town, settling our two older sons into new digs before the start of the university year. When she saw the dinky plane log standing where it was, I imagined she subtly rolled her eyes, although I'm probably being unkind. Like an upcountry *strandloper*, I was always bringing things home: lemons, mussel shells, strange-shaped bits of wood, water-polished stones – items for a modern-day still life. In time we would both forget about the plane log as it took its place among the much-loved flotsam of our lives until one night in winter I remembered and casually tossed it on the fire.

By the time we'd navigated past the snakes and slow charms of Vilakazi Street, it was late morning, and the entire township seemed to be out of doors. I crossed Elias Motsoaledi Road, heading towards the June 16 memorial. Life was busy here on Mphuthi Street, crowded, with the scurry of noise and life. Minibus taxis were stacked two and three deep around a corner, and I noticed a number of businesses housed in used containers. Pinky's Mobile Kitchen advertised its wares and, further along, Tiny's Investment Services. As I picked my

131

way between kerb and road I noticed that I was about to be caught in the middle of a funeral – or possibly two. Swanky mourners were sitting down on white plastic chairs, waiting to be served lunch by Pinky and her retainers, and there seemed to be another funeral on the go too, the bereaved and hangers-on ambling out of a church I sensed was close by but couldn't quite see. Cars were backed far up the street and traffic was inching slowly down the hill in search of parking. But it was good-natured congestion. I peered into gazebos and tents to see more. It was polite and ordered, a priest here, a congregation there. A group of middle-aged women in black and white (they might have been wearing berets) were in attendance and people slung themselves into chairs, taking the weight off their feet. I sensed an all-day affair, an eternity of waiting. As the throng thinned, I began to walk with slightly more freedom. Heading up the gentle hill, I greeted a group of women sipping shade beneath a large tree. No sooner had we said hello than one of them pushed a copy of *The Watchtower – Announcing Jehova's Kingdom* into my already occupied hand. I was beginning to feel slightly overburdened, what with my small log of plane, my notebook and my camera. As I walked, hands full, I was approached by a young mother, a baby cradled in a blanket on her back and a slightly older child walking alongside. He obviously wasn't looking, because the next thing I heard terrible tears. He hadn't been watching where he was going – he might have been watching me as he approached – and had accidentally walked straight into a pole.

I confess I didn't pay the attention that I should have on

the part of the route that followed. I looked emptily at the June 16 memorial and the installation further up Mphuthi Street. Both reminded me of Freedom Park in Pretoria, the same use of thin slices of layered stone, the same understated, calm aesthetic, low-slung, with abundant stone circles. There were photos mounted on poles with long explanatory captions – one read 'Gaps and Silences' – and I looked at them inattentively, slightly bored. I'd spent most of the walk bringing up the rear, sometimes shepherding Simon along, thinking, when we weren't walking together, how comfortable he must be in the SABC cameraman's car, and I was eager not to be left behind. It wasn't long before I spied my Mpanza Memorial Walk comrades up in front, turning towards what I presumed was the Oppenheimer Memorial and the Credo Mutwa Centre. Very soon, I reached the crest of the hill myself and made the turn, finding renewed energy now that my destination was in sight.

In 1954 Sir Ernest Oppenheimer of the Anglo American Corporation was invited to visit Soweto by Wilhelm Carr, the city council's manager of Non-European Affairs. Sir Ernest arrived in a chauffeur-driven Rolls Royce, with precious little clearance above the ground. The rutted roads of Soweto were not to the car's liking and soon the party transferred to Carr's less salubrious Ford, a vehicle with less room on the back seat but all-round higher clearance. They spent the morning visiting the Moroka shanty town, and although he was by nature a taciturn man, accounts of the visit indicate that Oppenheimer was moved by what he saw. Conditions were woeful: there was squalor, the standard issue of dormant water, mangy dogs and wood smoke. The council's house-building record was poor through the late 1940s and when the National Party came to power in 1948, building slowed even further. Almost immediately after his tour, Oppenheimer pledged R6 million to the city to be repaid over 30 years. The shanty town was immediately flattened and Oppenheimer's loan contributed to the building of nearly 15 000 houses in the Moroka area before the decade was out.

The Oppenheimer Tower was built in 1956 to commemorate Oppenheimer's generosity. It took six months to build and was made out of breeze blocks composed of slag and cinder from some of the demolished structures in the Moroka and Orlando West shanty town, the very settlement that Mpanza had urged the women to build in defiance of the authorities a decade before. It is a practical, almost timeless structure, built without flourish or frippery. For all that, it is strangely elegant, a cylinder tapering slightly from base to top. The tower emerges suddenly from the surrounding thorn bush and cabbage trees, almost like something that has descended from above rather than something that has been painstakingly built from below. Once you've climbed the 49 green steps you have 360-degree views of the city, from Baragwanath Hospital (once a motel, apparently) to Soweto's second hospital, which is almost directly opposite on the far western edge of the township. Look carefully with the help of a guide and you can spot Soweto's nearest theatre, the Orlando Stadium, from which we had walked, and a variety of landmarks and shrines to the struggle.

Thinking about it afterwards, I reflected that there was

something slightly wrong with the scene. Soweto has every-thing nowadays, ranging from modern shopping malls to car dealerships. Yet it has no commercial heart. What it really needs is its own stock exchange, an Old Mutual or Liberty Life head office, or maybe a regional centre for SABMiller. Without such institutions it looks like an increasingly well-provisioned dormitory town, a town whose purpose is to provide labour for headquarters elsewhere. It needs the credibility of such institutions, ones that might decide not to opt for Sandton or the Pinelands interchange but to plump for Soweto – and to do so because it makes both commercial and political sense.

At the foot of the Oppenheimer memorial is the Credo Mutwa Centre, a flaky amalgam of statues, icons and ron-davels illustrating Mutwa's cosmology. I read it as a kind of outdoor storybook, filled with ancestors and creatures from the seer's bombastic imagination. I wasn't surprised when I heard that Mutwa came from KwaZulu-Natal because many of the statues had a Hindu feel. I thought I saw Vishnu and perhaps the large head of Ganesha, the elephant. For all the evident mumbo-jumbo, it was an eclectic, busy space, with a sign at the entrance to the cultural village warning 'all liars, fools, sceptics and atheists to please keep out'. I probably failed on three of the four counts but wandered in regardless. I was careful not to remove anything or 'destroy any part of this place', for the sign also said that a seven-year curse would befall me if I did. Mostly I just wanted to sit down and catch my breath.

As I sat in the back of the taxi on our way back to Vuka's

place on Mooki Street, I wondered what the Credo Mutwa Centre reminded me of. The best I could come up with was Helen Martin's house in Nieu-Bethesda, full of concrete owls and strange anorexic shapes and structures. There was something obsessive in both spaces, and something lonely, as they carved out their respective visions against the terrible indifference of posterity, to bastardise a famous phrase by English historian E.P. Thompson. I haven't been able to quite get to grips with the story, but, apparently, Mutwa wasn't much liked by the schoolchildren of the '76 riots. He was seen as a Zulu traditionalist and purveyor of dingbat theories, and when he was allegedly misquoted in the Afrikaans press as a supporter of separate development, part of his village was burnt down. He suffered further depredations. In the 80s the cultural village was burnt yet again, part of strike action against the West Rand Administration Board. He lost his son in political violence and relocated to what was then Bophuthatswana, to continue his life's work as a prophet and sangoma. Most of all, I think, he would have seen himself as a folklorist – a librarian of the Zulu soul. He must have felt exposed, trying to preserve a culture smoothed and shaped by modern conveniences: photocopiers, then faxes, then emails and the internet. When faced with WhatsApp and Twitter, he would have known that he was taking a pitchfork into battle against cruise missiles.

Back at Vuka's house, I waited my turn to leave the taxi. As I clambered through the sliding doors in search of something cold to drink, a member of the Memorial Walk group hit me for the taxi fare. Other than greeting her that morning, we hadn't said a word to each other all day. She was dressed, I noticed, in the most recent gear – good takkies and a day-glo shirt – and didn't look short of cash. Tired, and not thinking clearly, I whipped the double fare out of my wallet. It was not the first time that day that I had been artfully relieved of an idea or a note. Perhaps I had just been exposed to the 'Soweto way' – although it was more likely that I had been trapped in a very South African dance. Let's call it the 'infinite rites of manipulation' and leave it at that.

7

'THERE WAS NO MAGIC ABOUT THE SHORTS'

Prieska Road, Makapanstad, North West,
via the Lutheran church to the house on stand
number 1 731 — about 2.5 kilometres

South African politics is full of stories of ordinary folk walking their grievances up to the gates of history. Some do so with noise and clamour; others with great discipline; others, still, walk serenely, going about their politics with an almost spectral calm. For a couple of years, from May 1910 until the end of 1912, Mahatma Gandhi lived on an ashram called Tolstoy Farm, south-west of what is present-day Lenasia, on land owned by his friend (and possible lover) Hermann Kallenbach. Inspired by Count Leo Tolstoy's dreams of agrarian self-sufficiency, Gandhi and his followers dug wells, and planted peach and almond trees. They looked at the stars, prayed to various Hindu gods and lived a life of noble, if muted, contemplation. From time to time they needed to dip into the messy waters of the world. Gandhi had a legal practice to support, so three times a week he woke in the middle of the night and walked from Tolstoy Farm past Langley Station and into Johannesburg, a distance of 30 kilometres, possibly slightly more. After a day's worth of legal work, which often consisted of helping and advising his Hindu countrymen, he turned around and headed back in the direction of home.

Fine-boned, jug-eared, ascetic, he levitates under a canopy of stars. His sandal-step is light, the touch of his staff soft. He leaves barely a footprint. Such quiet, obdurate steps tell the story of his life in the language of walking.

When Philip Ata Kgosana led a march of 30 000 mainly Xhosa migrant workers from the hostels of Langa to the Houses of Parliament in 1960, he walked in a more robust if slightly less comfortable fashion, his size-eight feet wedged into sockless size-five shoes. He had arrived at the University of Cape Town earlier that year, the beneficiary of an Institute of Race Relations bursary. They paid for his fees, not for books or living expenses or pocket money, and although he managed to scrounge the price of a third-class train ticket from Pretoria to Cape Town, his pockets were as empty as his stomach when finally he arrived. With an address in his palm, he made his way to District Six. He was fed and accommodated for a week but had to move on, finding his way to Langa and the men's hostels, a hotbed of anger and disaffection. He had seen Robert Sobukwe talk while at Lady Selborne High, the school from which he matriculated north of Pretoria, and his young heart was smitten with Sobukwe and his rejection of the hated pass books.

'I had a powerful impression of this fabulous man who could articulate his message with fantastic clarity,' Kgosana told me one muggy morning in February 2016. 'We, who were young and militant, were having problems with the way the ANC was conducting its business. One day we realised that the ANC's regular "stay-at-home" strike wasn't going to hurt. Sobukwe said: "When you are in a fight, hit the man beneath the belt so he can feel the pinch." That was what we liked to hear. Our problem was with the pass book. There was even talk at that time that our womenfolk were going to have to start carrying them too.'

In the wake of the Sharpeville Massacre, nine days before the march, many of the Pan Africanist Congress's (PAC) senior leaders were either in prison or on the run. So it fell to the 23-year-old Kgosana to lead the masses to Roeland Street Police Station on 30 March 1960. This he did with a gravity and discipline that might strike us as almost improbable today. As former *New York Times* correspondent in South Africa, Joseph Lelyveld recounts in his fine book *Move Your Shadow*, all contemporary accounts of the march, from witnesses, participants and newspaper reports, agree that those who marched were ordered and dignified – in a phrase, well-mannered. According to what Kgosana told a post-march commission of inquiry, as reported in Lelyveld's book: 'When I told them [the marchers] to sit down, they sat down. When I told them to stand up, they stood up. When I ordered them to go back quietly, they went back quietly.'

As I walked with Kgosana that sticky February day in his home village of Makapanstad, north-west of Pretoria, I found myself searching for ways to describe him. He was impish and charmingly old-school, using words like 'fellows', 'gentlemen' and 'womenfolk'. At one point in our ramble he stopped and delicately announced that he 'needed to pass water'.

Eventually, I stumbled upon a description: he was almost regal, a refugee from a more courtly age. This might have had something to do with the influence of parents and church on the generation in which he grew up, we agreed, and their stress on discipline, dignified toil and etiquette. Here was a man who came from a Bible-reading, highly religious family. Eloquence was important. He remembers reading Shakespeare and Jane Austen at school, as well as the Setswana novel *Mokwena* by D.P. Moloto. He even remembers the authors of his Senior Certificate history textbook – Fowler and Smit. These were cherished, like family heirlooms. Learning, wisdom, eloquence: here were verities worth striving for.

There was also a deep pool of racial memory to dip into and a surprisingly nurturing local community. Place was important to Kgosana: the Waterberg, Winterveldt, Soshanguve, Makapanstad – the history of his family moved through them all like cattle through grass. The flat plains stretching north of Pretoria to the foothills of the Waterberg had been converted by his family, his forebears and his community into a place of memory and a deep well of meaning – a spiritual wonderland capable of infinite replenishment. To these gentle lands Kgosana returned home after 30 years in exile, tending the family farm with the profound satisfaction that follows homecoming. 'When I was in Uganda you used to see professional men in Kampala – surgeons, doctors – heading out into the countryside of a weekend,' he told me. 'They would spend a few nights and return to the city on a Sunday, their boots full of yams and produce. You don't see that very much here.'

Another answer to the question of Kgosana's bearing might be found in a story he told as we ambled down the hamlet's gravel roads. When he was in matric at Lady Selborne, awakening to the wider world through teachers like Nathaniel Masemola and Bob Letshwai, his father announced that he was going to Bon Accord Farm to buy a horse. *'Bobbejaan, watter perd soek jy,'* asked the farmer when Philip and his father arrived in search of a mare. Matters continued in this vein for several minutes, the white farmer continuing to refer to Philip's father as a baboon. Eventually the young man could stand it no longer. 'I lost control and went for the farmer,' he told me. 'My father stepped between us and got in the way. We avoided what would have been a terrible situation. There was silence on the journey home. When we returned to my mother he told her that I didn't agree with a black man being called a baboon. What right did I, a young boy, have to such thoughts? Men like the farmer should always be obeyed. That was simply the way things were.'

Finding fault with such logic, the young Kgosana orbited in wider and wider arcs from his father's light. He was forced to grow up, to think independent thoughts, becoming a man before others in less straitened circumstances might have reached adulthood. He originally wanted to study pharmacy at university, then flirted with medicine. Finally he was persuaded by his brother to take an economics degree because it had commercial application. Seeking to escape his father's influence was often more difficult than he thought. When Philip picked his way through Woodstock in search of a small printing works to publish PAC pamphlets and literature, he discovered that his father had lived in the suburb before him, studying building and carpentry. For seven years he learnt his trade, returning to build many of Makapanstad's early structures, like the Church of Christ, in which he later preached as leader of a transplanted American apostolic church. Today the rectangular shed is a sad structure, full of cobwebs and crumbling plaster. It contains some rickety benches, some stacked plastic chairs and a few primary-school desks with inkwells and lids. The only concessions to style or beauty are a few long windows down the side wall, which might once have had a pane of stained glass or two in them, I couldn't be sure. The floor was so dusty, I noticed, that it had subtly changed colour, and was now a gentle cinnamon. Despite all this, Kgosana senior was nothing if not practical. The house in which Philip grew up and the Church of Christ stand side by side. All he needed to do on Sunday mornings was roll out of bed and climb the pulpit.

For all his manly striving, in other ways Philip was still a boy. Photographs of the march show him moon-faced, almost chubby, his features beatifically soft. He didn't own a car, being too poor, and on the day of the march he caught an early ride in the car of a correspondent for the *Christian Science Monitor*. He didn't have a girlfriend or more than a pound and 15 shillings to his name when he arrived in the Cape. This prompted him to write in my notebook (because I was driving and didn't want to forget the splendid cadence of his words): 'It was then I realised the story of my grim situation.' His too-small shoes were cut in such a way as to accommodate his toes, and his jacket was a gift from his former headmaster at Lady Selborne. Best of all, he led the march wearing a pair of black hand-me-down short pants, like an Edwardian schoolboy hero. 'There was no magic about the shorts,' this proto-*kortbroek* told Lelyveld, 'except that they tell an untold story that at that time I did not have many clothes to wear.'

Kgosana was again wearing shorts on the day of our walk, pedal pushers, a bright Hawaiian shirt and a triangular sedge hat bought while on holiday in China. We started at the intersection of Prieska Road and Makapanstad's main street, Philip pointing out that the area hereabout was called 'Majakaneng' or 'place of the converts'. This, he explained, was because many of the Kgosanas who owned houses here – including his father's uncle, Willem, and Willem's son, Lucky – had converted to Christianity. Most notable of these converts was Jacob Phake Kgosana, Philip's great-grandfather, who arrived from the Waterberg about a hundred years ago and promptly became a Lutheran. So literal was his faith that he went to church with a lamb. 'The lamb was so trained that it waited for him,' Philip told me, explaining that although the family knew Jacob had been buried in 1920, they didn't know exactly where, so we tottered along to the old Lutheran Cemetery. As we did, Philip explained that Lutheran records in the Magaliesburg had been consulted and how, eventually, the grave had been located. A headstone erected in 1993 makes reference to 'the great elephant' – the elephant being the family totem. The reference clearly gives Philip a great deal of pleasure.

As we crept into the graveyard, swinging the gate before

us, we noticed a group of five gravediggers, taking turns with a pick and shovel beneath a thorn tree, a pile of paprika-red earth alongside. According to Philip, they are called *Diphiri*, or wolves, in Tswana, presumably because wolves once raided cemeteries in search of meat or bones. We walked around, with not a tree in sight, all gravel, rusted fencing and a sea of headstones. As we picked our way towards the centre of the cemetery I began to notice teapots. There were hundreds of them, of all descriptions. China ones, enamel ones, dusty buttery yellows and faded orange pots with feathery spouts. Best of all was one of those cream-coloured institutional monsters with green rims and tips, the kind of teapot you might once have found in a government depart-ment or mental institution. Along with the teapots, some of them now lolling on the ground after having fallen off the graves, were cups and saucers, plates and mugs. It was like stumbling into a crockery department in Garlicks or Stutta-fords, except that everything was rusted or broken or chipped. It soon became clear that these were votive offerings, ar-ranged to placate the ancestors. They were saying: 'We hope you accept our sacrifice and don't bother us', although they might also have been a welcome back, just in case the ances-tors felt lonely and decided to pop in for tea.

Our next port of call was the Lutheran church, built in 1913 by locals and Lutheran missionaries. The Lutherans had clearly been here for far longer because a simple painting on one of the inside church walls recorded 10 names of those baptised in 1868. It was not until many years later that this poor community managed to pool enough funds for a structure they would be proud of. Even so, there were clearly some building and architectural issues. The bell is not accommodated in the structure of the church but by an elongated steel frame outside, and the church itself has the rustic, primitive feel of one built by zealous amateurs on a shoe-string budget. The roof is made of red tin, the pews are basic and the stained glass thin and without radiance. The Kgosana family's reach extended even here. According to Philip, his father used the training he had gained in Woodstock to carve the steps winding up to the pulpit as well as the pulpit itself. Buried in the cemetery nearby are three members of the same missionary family – Albert, Elizabeth and Anna Hacke – who clearly played important everyday roles in the church too. Albert died at 48, Elizabeth lived until she was 68, but Anna, their daughter, was the most tragic of all. She was 15 when she died in 1941, a girl. *Auf wiedersehn droben!* reads the inscription on one of their graves, somehow sadder for its cheery attempt at upliftment.

Maybe it was time spent as a boy in the Lutheran church, a church his father helped to build, that fortified Philip spiritually that March day in 1960. As the marchers' snaked along De Waal Drive and descended into the city bowl, curtains were quietly drawn, and doors locked and bolted. There was a helicopter hovering overhead and armed men were lounging watchfully on armoured cars parked along the route. Having left their pass books behind, the protesters sang joyfully – songs like *'Unzima lomtwalo'* ('This burden is heavy') and *'Tina sizwe e sintsundu'*, a lament over land lost to the colonialists. The mood was cheery, the sun shone. Discipline, as ever, was good. As the march approached Roeland Street Police Station and the gates of Parliament beyond, Lelyveld reminds us that this was the stupendously unlikely moment when a fresh-faced 23-year-old suddenly became the most important person among millions of disenfranchised black South Africans. Sobukwe had already handed himself over to the authorities in Orlando and although Albert Luthuli, the Methodist lay preacher and then head of the ANC, had publicly burnt his pass book in the days following Sharpeville, the hotline to the soul of the black masses was the PAC's. 'For a period that can be measured in minutes rather than hours,' writes Lelyveld, 'Philip Kgosana appears to have held the fate of his country in his hand as no other black man has before or since. There can be no doubt that if he had ordered the crowd to march the final few blocks to Parliament, it would have marched, whatever the consequences.'

Consequences there were – although, fortunately, they weren't as bloody or dramatic as what had happened at Sharpeville. Sobukwe had always stressed non-violence. In a memorable phrase, there was to be 'no leading of corpses to a new Africa'. He didn't want the rank and file to become 'cannon fodder', he wrote to the PAC leadership in a smuggled speech. When Kgosana realised that Parliament was guarded by armed policemen, he ordered the marchers to halt. From the moment he raised his hand, ordering calm and dignity as he asked the phalanx to stop, the entire city must have retreated in fear. These men, however, were not a mob. They regathered, turned around and marched back from where they had come. Having asked to see the Minister of

Justice, Kgosana was told curtly that 'he was out to lunch' and was summarily imprisoned.

Amid widespread intimidation and brutality, the strike, of which the march was part, was stomped out. Lelyveld writes of the glint of bayonets shimmering in the darkness around Langa and Nyanga, the most militant townships, on the nights following the march. The authorities cut off the townships' water and electricity. Within days, the strike had been put down. An uneasy calm returned to the peninsula.

On Christmas Eve 1960, Kgosana slipped out of the country, never finishing the degree he had started at the beginning of the year. He didn't tell his parents, only his brother. He took nearly four agonising months to wind his way to Tanzania. The message conveyed to PAC members from Sobukwe in prison was that military training was necessary because the organisation had been further broken by the imprisonment of its leaders. The Nationalist government promulgated a raft of draconian new laws and Sobukwe now believed armed struggle was inevitable. As Kgosana wound his way further up the east coast of Africa, he finally joined an Ethiopian paratrooper regiment, jumping six times, securing his wings and becoming an officer before enrolling in university. Hurling himself out of a transport aircraft was counter-intuitive, Kgosana admitted, and while he was not overly enamoured with Ethiopia or Ethiopians, he told me, he nonetheless made it his temporary base and managed to eke out an existence. He was married there in 1967 and started a family. His degree paved the way for employment and Lelyveld tracked him down in Colombo, Sri Lanka, in the mid-80s,

where he worked for UNICEF. Lelyveld conducted inter-
views, with Philip sending back his replies by cassette. In
Move Your Shadow, Lelyveld notes 'the sombre, sad cadences'
of a man only partly reconciled to a life of permanent exile.
At 79, I found a man far older but one who had come home
to the land in which he will be buried. Despite his advancing
age, he was considerably perkier than I imagined him to be
when answering Lelyveld's questions. More than that, he was
still vibrating with energy. He had plans and views. Life wasn't
over by a long chalk.

The final terminus on our ramble through the houses,
sheds and pondoks of Makapanstad was the house in which
Philip had grown up, number 1 731 on the street-with-no-
name. It was a simple, flat-roofed affair, with two outside
rooms creating space for a covered stoep or porch between
them. The house was guarded by several recently pruned
indigenous trees at the front and a deftly ornamental front
gate with what looked like a cross set into its middle and a
border of small tridents pointing skywards on top. Philip
introduced himself and chatted to the group of amiable old
men who now seemed to live there. Like many rural men of
a certain generation, they were proud yet suffused with a
certain bowed heaviness. Philip dusted off the charm and I
smiled and felt slightly spare as he spoke to them in the
vernacular. I wandered off, down gravel lanes, past houses
where mangy dogs were tethered in ungrassed yards. It was
a different world here in Makapanstad – humble but cared-
for, clean, the potholes filled with bricks and mortar, the
gravel yards showing telltale signs of being swept with

makeshift brooms. A group of labourers in blue overalls were mending Philip's roof, pulling out rotting rafters and replacing them with fresher timber. Folk were tinkering with cars or hanging out washing. At one point around the grave-yard earlier we had heard the jolly tune of an approaching walker. He continued whistling as he walked past, bow-legged, a curious madness burning in his orange eyes. Here was a man who walked through history, through literature, through time. Chaucer might have seen him as his 28 pilgrims left the clutches of Southwark as they pounded the turnpike for Canterbury. I had seen this fellow before, we all have. He was both man and ghost, happily haunted, and walking for all he was worth.

As we looped back to where I had parked my car, Philip persuaded me to take a quick drive to his farm. It wasn't far away, he said, and we drove off, down dusty lanes marked with turn-offs to Jericho and Hebron. After half an hour we arrived at a homestead, a simple house with several big, airy rooms and a succession of outbuildings, one of which con-tained mushrooms, Philip told me. The farm was not a big one, containing just under 2 000 trees. Most of these were citrus trees but about 700 were transplanted African trees called moringas. Kgosana had seen these in Uganda for the first time and eulogised about their energy-boosting pro-perties. 'The leaves are dried for powder and capsules,' he said, 'and you can make tea bags and soap. Moringa treats diabetes and cures high blood pressure. It was even used in the fight against HIV/Aids in Uganda.'

As Philip was talking to a scythe-wielding foreman, I pottered about, noticing an old borehole pump house in a brick shed. I walked between ripening rows of valencias, navels, naartjies and lemons, straw mulch surrounding their base to prevent evaporation. As I watched Philip's interaction with his foreman, I sensed that he didn't seem to be quite as welcome on his land as he ought to be. Still, I reflected, it was his and, as such, was the wellspring of his identity. His farm, he told me later, was one of 163 black-owned local citrus farms in a cradle across the Winterveldt joined in a cooperative. What Philip called an 'anchor farm' was the main producer and farms like his provided only a small percentage of the cooperative's harvest but they were more protected from the vagaries of the market by being a collective. He had plans, he added, to sink another borehole. With more water he could provide irrigation for more trees. A bush-clearing programme was about to begin. Such were an old man's vivid dreams of expansion.

As I drove Philip back to his home in Pretoria North, I reflected on the slightly strained atmosphere I sensed back at the farm. Part of me was hoping for a cup of tea, some famed Winterveldt hospitality. Then I'd remembered what I'd seen: a vat of sunflower oil on the Formica-topped kitchen table, three medium-sized onions in a sad still life alongside. This is what Philip's tenants had by way of supplies. They had nothing to offer, I realised, because they had nothing to give.

8

THE MAN WHO DRAPED HIS JACKET OVER THE ALEXANDRA DAM WALL

Constantia Nek via the Overseer's Cottage
and the five Table Mountain dams to the
remains of the Kasteelpoort Aerial Cableway
and back again — about 15 kilometres

Having climbed about 200 metres above the Constantia Nek parking lot, I stopped to gather my breath. Summer was creeping from the trees far below, pools of soft yellows and dying greens so various they were difficult to describe. It wasn't only happening in Tokai and Constantia. Braaing outside one evening before I left Joburg, I was amazed to hear the sound of nearby popping – I couldn't quite pinpoint from where. The sound was somewhere above me, deep in the trees. It was happening regularly, perhaps in response to the falling temperature, but without rhythm. I listened again. It wasn't mechanical and it wasn't that familiar sound of a close-but-faraway woodpecker; neither was it the crazed hammering of a young barbet who often attacked his reflection in a window pane. I sipped my beer, chuckled at my inability to trace the sound, and wondered if I was going slightly mad. Perhaps invisible children were lobbing acorns onto our tin roof? No, that wasn't right, but what was it? What on earth could it be? After another puzzled sip, I stalked the sound. The furious pop was coming from splitting wisteria pods, releasing the last of their summer seeds as they fell to the ground. I bent down to examine one: the outer pod was covered in an almost velvet-like skin of olive-green. Inside, the dark wisteria seeds were housed in perfect white hollows like sleepy toddlers eased into a duvet. Back in September I'd started my walk in Pringle country by describing the first heavy fumbling of spring. Now the great river of summer was slowing, dispersing at its end. Up in the darkening sky, the leaves of the stinkwood close to the wisteria were creaking closed like halves of a clam. The walnuts were stretching open their thick green jackets, a sure sign of ripening. Soon our wintertime companions, the rats, would be scrambling for the warmth of the roof.

Autumn was less obvious up on Table Mountain. The fynbos carried on regardless, a kingdom of exquisite miniatures, almost bonsai-like, all delicate pinks and rich reds. I began to notice tiny yellow daisies popping up in the grass that grew between the tracks as I slogged upwards, sometimes on gravel, sometimes on the edge of the concrete slab. In places, dogs had walked in the drying concrete where the jeep track had been repaired. There was something sadly comical about the trail of prints, here one moment, gone the next. I thought about them and why they touched me as they did, as I paused to admire the view. My eye travelled south-east across False Bay to Rooi Els and the faraway pincer of Cape Hangklip. In the middle distance were the cool waterways of Marina da Gama and the bustle of the Muizenberg coast. East of that was the sprawl of the Flats, a milky haze lingering in the air. The morning was still, the few clouds high and silent. It was a wonderful day for a hike.

As I gasped for the summit after about an hour of hard walking, I was passed by about 10 old Mountain Clubbers rolling off the mountain. They were sun-flushed and chirpy, well kitted out in hats and good boots. Two or three pulled themselves along with ski poles. They gave off a good aura, something beyond conviviality or happiness. It had to do with shared experience and made them quietly buoyant, as if they were levitating. As they passed, I heard the bubble of several conversations and then they were gone, spirited away, as if by magic.

Before long I saw the first of the five dams – De Villiers – off to my left. The water level was low, and directly above the high-water mark you could see the almost-white rock of the original dam wall, preserved by the tannin-coloured properties of what was usually a higher water level. The final stripe was almost black, a combination of lichen, pollution and everyday corrosion, but my eye kept on returning to examine the whiteness of the band beneath. This was how it would have pretty much looked when it was built over 100 years ago, the final stone being laid by Sir John Henry de Villiers and various Wynberg councillors in February 1910. It was a glimpse into another time, rare and thrilling. The dog prints were of the same register – traces of what once was, a world gone forever. I am sometimes chilled to wordlessness by such things, yet cannot grope towards understanding with anything but words. The idea that this is all lost, that there were once lives here, and dreams and beating hearts, is sometimes too much for my soul to bear. I think, as I write this, that we might all be born with something like millennial grief. I suspect that I could be more predisposed than others to experiencing it, but certain landscapes surely lend themselves to such feelings more than others. The top-of-the-mountain tableland, a sort of beautiful outdoor reliquary, full of industrial abandonment and forgotten voices, brought my grief full to the surface. I walked with it as a companion throughout the day.

* * *

When seen from above, the five dams of what is called the Back Table are not dissimilar in shape to a gigantic question mark, with De Villiers Dam forming the mark's full stop, angled slightly off to one side. Above that, in the main body of the mark, are Alexandra and Victoria dams and, higher still, Hely-Hutchinson and Woodhead. Named after queens, worthies and mayors, the dams were all built between 1890 and 1910, a response to the growing realisation on the part of City of Cape Town officials that demand for water would soon outstrip supply, a conclusion sharpened by the fact that the middle years of the 1890s were unusually dry ones. Table Mountain and its slopes are, in fact, a network of pipes, tunnels, pump stations and reservoirs. The Woodhead Tunnel, for example, takes water flowing in the Disa River and shoots it off the Back Table above the kramats south of Bakoven. The water is then channelled back towards Camps

Bay along a contour path. If you walk the pipe track (in the opposite direction) from Kloof Nek, you often walk beside these pipes as they transport water via a filtration plant, around the Nek and into the Molteno Reservoir in Oranje- zicht. After the tunnel was built, it was embarrassingly realised that the Disa often dried up in summer. The Wood- head Dam was therefore built to supply regular water for the tunnel, which, in turn, fed the Molteno Reservoir, and not the other way round.

Some of the toil and ingenuity that these engineering feats demanded is captured in an album of old black-and-white photographs in the South African Museum, in the Company Gardens. One photograph stands out. It is taken from close to where the Kloof Nek wash houses are today, and shows Lion's Head in the background. In the foreground is a staging post or temporary camp. We see several two-wheeled trolleys or carts upon which rest a solid wooden base or platform. On this platform lies a massive steel pipe, several metres long. The trolleys have been hauled by faceless teams of African labourers. They all wear gigantic hats and the ropes they've been pulling lie curled at their feet. A growing stack of pipes stands next to them in open veld like so many cannon barrels, and everywhere is the spool of dust, flattened grass and industry, the sharp bite of the African sun on what I would guess is a hot January or February day. A couple of grim Victorian gentlemen with impressive moustaches are stand- ing around, supervising matters. They are wearing pith helmets and breeches, and are dressed as if for hunting or exploration. In some photos they have brought their dogs.

The labour segment between the unsmiling British engineers and the slaves was occupied by professional working men. These were often Welsh or Cornish miners induced to the Cape in search of opportunities just like this. They dug the Woodhead Tunnel and ferried out the rock in cocopans. They also built the brick aqueducts that supported the pipe, clean and neat and expressive of an age when masons and dressers of stone were not far removed from artists.

Each dam has its own shape, design and engineering challenges, although all are broadly similar. Looking down off the De Villiers Dam wall, for example, there appear to be what look like four stone hinges at the base of the wall. They almost look like the flying buttresses one sees in medieval cathedrals, except they're far smaller, acting as covers, perhaps, for run-off to a small pump house nearby and ultimately down into an indigenous forest on the Hout Bay side of the mountain below. For some unknown reason – perhaps it was the microclimate or the rays of the sun – the dam wall on this side is generally cleaner and appears to have weathered better than the other walls that I looked at deeper into my walk. On closer inspection, I also noticed that the cleanest part of the dam wall on the water side wasn't entirely white. It was mostly white, sometimes darkening to a gentle cinnamon or biscuit colour. Still, all these dams were handsome structures, built with what I can only describe as love by the masons and engineered with grave, clean dignity by a Scottish civil engineer called Thomas Stewart.

It is not only the gentle curve of the dam walls that captures the imagination. Further along, past the Overseer's Cottage (and its wild sprawl of button-sized stone roses growing outside) and up a gentle incline lies Alexandra Dam and, head to tail, as it were, Victoria Dam beyond that. You are not meant to swim in these dams or drink their water, the colour of Fanta Orange, but at the thinnest point of Victoria – its ankle, you might say – I stopped to drink and unwrap a sweet. I found a comfortable rock, enjoyed the shade it provided, and looked east towards the dam wall. Beyond the wall, my eye fell onto the top peaks of the Hottentots Holland range on the other side of False Bay, some 50 kilometres away. I sensed that all the dams were built like this. They were built according to the sturdy principles of functionality but there was always something aesthetically satisfying about them, some soft nod or acknowledgement to the beauty of form. Beyond that they often snagged in the land in such a way so as not to dwarf the broader environment – and what rose and fell all around. Like an excessively polite visitor loath to intrude, they were not meant to draw attention to themselves. In their restraint and proportion, however, they did the very opposite of what perhaps was intended. You wanted to look again, or look more carefully. It was not only an exercise in watching time up here but it was a long seminar in aesthetics. These dams demanded that you look with hunger, almost acquisitively, and when you had looked for a long while you looked some more.

Once I was up on the Back Table proper, the walking was level and easy. There were no trees up here except for the odd spreadeagled old pine. The fynbos was fragrant and delicate. There were bulrushes and small shrubs, all tiny-leaved and looking vaguely medicinal. This for lumbago, I could imagine some wise Noordhoek hippy telling me, an infusion of this for heart-sickness. Drink tea of such-and-such for ailments of the liver and spleen. A poultice of this for flowery language, perhaps, and this for the writer who suffers from the curse of taking himself too seriously. I busied along, eager for the next dams, the star attractions – Woodhead and Hely-Hutchinson. I wasn't disappointed, although best of all were not the dams themselves but the walk between them. You can thread a path at the foot of the Hely-Hutchinson, looking to your left at the wind-ruffled surface of the Wood-head, her dark waters somehow grave and weighty. Up to your right, rising up like the cliff of a canyon is the Hely-Hutchinson wall, bowed and, at eye level, busy with moss, lichen, calcium stains and leaks. As I turned around to draw a brick weir in my notebook, I noticed a black grass snake seeping ghost-like into its hole. A chill brushed over me. The weir and outlet canal were magnificent, made of the same dressed stone as the dams and quarried nearby. There were weeds and grasses growing in its cracks now but there was something monumental here, and so pleasing. A vision per-haps or at least a philosophy. It made me want to know more about Stewart and the men who laid every lump of stone, each one painstakingly dressed, each one subtly different.

As I walked through the non-existent shadow of the dam wall (I somehow imagine, now, in recollection, that there was shadow), I noticed that each block of stone had a depression in it, like a belly-button. Each small hollow was equidistant from the long sides, and no matter what the dimensions or shape of the block it was almost always in the same place. As I examined a block of stone, my eye passed upwards to something snagging on the edge of my peripheral vision. Two large crows were standing imperiously on the dam wall railings. Seen from below, they looked large and unusually menacing. Later in the afternoon, as I climbed off the mountain, I noticed them again, tumbling carelessly above the slopes. There were now three and they played in the wind without care or sorrow. 'Listening to the crows and wind,' I remember texting my wife, now that the cellphone signal was restored as I edged off the Back Table after nearly six hours' walking to the Constantia Nek parking lot.

Beyond the far edge of the Hely-Hutchinson reservoir wall (to judge from the inlaid plaques on the walls they are properly called reservoirs) is a small waterworks museum, now closed. The museum is surrounded by steam cranes with massive blackened boilers and large pieces of heavy machinery, wheels and bogies. I struggled to read the maker's name on the crane, but could just make out the words 'J.M. Wilson and Company, Liverpool'. I walked around, peering through the windows and reading the artefacts' captions upside down. There was a carbide miner's lamp, some old-fashioned scales and a ship's bell: 'This was mounted outside the resident engineer's office above the Woodhead Reservoir. (This later became the Waterworks Overseer's home.) The bell was used to ring out the daily working hours during the construction of the two dams.'

Pride of place in the museum goes to a small narrow-gauge steam engine imported from Kilmarnock in Scotland.

Material, including cement in casks, also imported from Scotland, was initially transported from the Kasteelpoort Aerial Cableway in miniature trucks pulled by mules. Later, the engine was imported, dismantled at the foot of the cableway and then reassembled once the parts had reached the top. The route it followed from the edge of the mountain can be walked from the waterworks museum, past the stone quarry and behind the Mountain Club hut, which occupies a bluff overlooking the Woodhead Dam. Continue further past the three old pines, and the jeep track seems to follow almost perfectly the curve of what was once the railway line. You can see the rubble-raised corners and the straights. Alongside the track are slightly raised concrete platforms, now weathered and overgrown with bushes and fynbos. Worker compounds were apparently erected on these platforms. There was even a kraal for animals. Workers, including the Cornish masons, Welsh miners and Pondo labourers, lived here for about three years, as did Stewart, living on this subtle tableland as he supervised the completion of the Woodhead. Today there is evidence everywhere of human habitation – some of it fairly recent. There are three or four old boarded-up houses and a cloying air of gentle melancholy. At the end of a slight curve, with the Atlantic glistening at your feet, are the remnants of the Kasteelpoort Aerial Cableway. Not much remains. There is a rectangular stone blockhouse, which was probably used to house the winching equipment, and you can see holes in the walls through which the cable wire passed. Peer over the edge and you can see old timber slats bolted into the rock face. These were probably used to anchor or direct the cables – possibly to protect them. Looking about, hearing the surge of the wind in your ears, it is impossible not to marvel at the mad audacity of what you have just seen. It all has a slight sandcastles-in-the-sand type feel. Soon enough, a final high tide is going to wash away the last remains for ever.

There is a photograph loitering on the internet of Stewart and a colleague being pulled up from Camps Bay in the Kasteelpoort lift. The men are close to the top and both look upwards, directly at the camera, neither looking happy. It's not entirely surprising: the lift or basket amounts to nothing more than a rudimentary cage with wooden planks for a floor. One can imagine the horror of a wind-buffeted descent or the awkwardness of having to share the limited space with some small but vital piece of equipment. Still, such journeys might have been relatively infrequent, because Stewart spent all of the three years required to build the Woodhead with his engineers and labourers up on the mountain. By the time the Hely-Hutchinson was needed, however, he'd had enough and decided to get married, spending most of his time in the suburbs below. Trips onto the Back Table became rare. Having recommended several good sites for natural catchment closer to the Constantia Nek side of the mountain, he might even have decided to have walked the route that I just had – climbing onto the Back Table via the zigzag path and the jeep track from the Constantia Nek saddle.

Although it is a beautiful structure, the Woodhead Dam's contribution to solving Cape Town's water problems was negligible. At the end of the 1890s, the demand for water from the city and its adjoining municipalities (like Wynberg) had spiked. There were various reasons for this state of affairs. The upgrade and extension of the local sewerage scheme demanded far more water than had hitherto been the case. Winter rains were also poor during the immediately preceding period, and there was an influx of visitors, soldiers and refugees because of the upcountry Boer War. Folk were clearly drinking themselves silly. This being the case, the authorities impressed upon Stewart the need for another dam, and this became the Hely-Hutchinson, built with largely the same crew, living in the original compound. 'As a matter of practical importance the construction [of Hely-Hutchinson] could be carried out from the existing camp,' he wrote in a report to the council, noting that after surveying the area once again, he had identified locations for further dams. In time, these became the Victoria, Alexandra and De Villiers dams, all three serving the flush and bumptious Wynberg Municipality, which had yet to be incorporated into the greater Cape Town metropole.

After inspecting the Kasteelpoort structure, I walked back towards the Mountain Club hut, tugging down on my cap every so often to prevent it from being blown off my head. I'd frozen water overnight and now downed what remained, nestling into a perfect hollow between two craggy pine roots as I sat down to munch nuts and dried pears. Up above, the pine branches creaked and drifted in the wind, and I sunk into bliss. As I sat in this perfect chair and ate in this perfect outdoor restaurant, I cast an eye over my immediate surroundings. Off to my right, a couple of metres away, there was a patch of grass that looked almost level enough to accommodate my tent. I fantasised about whether I would get away with it. My morning had been dogged by a white Cape Nature bakkie nosing along the jeep track to open sluices and transport hikers' equipment to and from the Overseer's Cottage, rented out to groups for the night. They had passed me four or five times and might head this way again, although I somehow doubted it. At nightfall, having made sure the mountain was empty, I'd pitch my tent, haul out some boerewors or steak, build the small fire that, if found, would see me fined or imprisoned.

Of course, I did nothing of the sort. I finished my supplies, becoming just slightly morose as I realised what I could have been eating. In my mind's eye I conjured up a fresh white roll, fat with cheese and mayonnaise. I was happy and relaxed and content yet I was also none of these things because, as I heaved a final handful of raw nuts into my mouth, I was dissatisfied. No, I was more than that: I was discontented. Indeed, I was sinking – quite rapidly – into a little strop of discontent. I was spoiled, I knew it. I was also, more importantly, underprepared. Our sons were always laughing at what they saw as my hopeless propensity for thrift, which manifested itself most obviously in undercatering. Now I was undercatering for myself. This was emotional terrorism of the worst kind. There are those who cater well and are therefore happy, which was my homespun version of René Descartes's famous dictum. Yet here I was, undercatered for and therefore unhappy. It was the perfect booby trap because

I could do nothing about it either, which made me realise that I must – at some level – like being unhappy. Perhaps even being unhappy, perversely, made me happy, although, of course, we could spin this out in a different way, which was that being unhappy, given that I had undercatered, simply deepened my unhappiness. This was a sobering thought, a more sobering thought than the relatively straightforward recognition that I had undercatered. Was this the perfect definition of the postmodern condition – the idea that even in our quiet reveries, the rare periods in which we are at our most content and happy, we are, in fact, unhappy, and unhappy for no more compelling reason than we are forever wanting what we can't and don't have. So that's it, is it? Our post-industrial, privileged lives are no more than high-wire balancing acts, with the possibility of happiness stretched thinly before us and the great chasm of unhappiness beckoning everywhere else. Maybe such feelings aren't confined to our current epoch. Perhaps all people, across time, have lusted after what they can't have, for this is what differentiates the human from the animal. It seems that animals are at one with their appetites, whereas we humans are never spiritually reconciled. We are forever snagged on the horns of better alternatives, always having to deal with the worm of dissatisfaction. Yet was this quite right? I was behaving pretty much like an animal now, wasn't I, worrying about base instincts, like hunger? I might have been trapped in the Escher-like stairway of my own thoughts but, at the instinctual level, I was still an animal. Perhaps this was it – we were all unhappy animals, were we not?

Despite my feelings of being hard done by food-wise, I realised that as I packed up and resumed my way, I was boundlessly and stupidly happy. As I started my gentle downward climb, I noticed that the lunchtime heat was softened by a growing wind. I walked back towards the gorgeous bow of a footpath at the base of the Hely-Hutchinson Dam wall and looked around with renewed vigour. I passed wild geranium. The flowers were mauve and everywhere the geranium's leaves were dusted with a furzy down. I marvelled at their hardy longevity and skipped on, noticing that clouds were now scudding in from the south-west. More and more of them poured in as the afternoon shadows grew longer, and eventually they covered the Silvermine mountains with a shifting blanket of cloud. As I walked past the Hely-Hutchinson wall, I noticed that water was being released into the Woodhead through a masonry culvert. It was folding at my feet, frothing in great creamy bubbles like freshly poured Guinness, as it made its way through marshy ground and eventually into the shallow reaches of its partner dam alongside. I barrelled on, walking briskly. There was no one on the mountain any more, and I had it all to myself. I walked brazenly into the cloud-littered afternoon.

Before long, I came alongside the two middle dams. I wasn't entirely sure, but one of the old black-and-white photographs I'd seen on an earlier trip to the National Library showed the workings on either the Alexandra or Victoria Dam wall. Above the dam wall, supported by a lattice of pine slats, was a substantial wooden bridge. The tracks held a steam crane, which ran to and fro on rails approximately the length of the

wall itself. Below the dam wall was another set of rails, supporting a rudimentary platform upon which rested a second,
less powerful crane or winch. The dam wall, growing upwards and surprisingly thick, stretched between the upper
and lower railway lines. According to some of the research
I had done, the dam walls were often filled with rubble
masonry, then 'faced with dressed stone'. This one must have
been 10 metres thick, so comfortable that it supported loads
of recently quarried rock, as well as two large groups of
workers. I noticed that a couple of labourers had removed
their dark jackets and had hung them casually over the top
of the dam wall. Looking more carefully still, I noticed that
one mason was in the midst of draping his jacket over the
dam wall as the photograph was being taken. He was wearing
a hat and his face was shrouded in shadow, but the act was
unmistakable. These were days before the advent of institutional uniforms and overalls, when men wore waistcoats, hats
and jackets to work. Who was this refugee from the gloom
of the past? How exactly did his labours have an impact on
the project and its completion? I couldn't help myself, and
ached to know more. Where was he from? What were his
loves and private reveries? Placing a jacket on a dam wall
was an act so careful, so intimately human, that I found it
touching. The dams were all named and celebrated, Stewart
and his fellow engineers feted and recognised, but who speaks
for the massed dignity of the casually forgotten? Who lights
a candle for the nameless man in the black hat placing his
jacket on a dam wall in an act so everyday that he did it both
carefully and without thought. Where did he go to when he

got off the mountain? I imagine he had his boots shined, afterwards sauntering into an Adderley Street bar, where the barman pulled him a pint. With a steady hand he took his drink to a quiet table, the quietest corner of the bar. He sipped from the beer's head, took out paper and a fountain pen from his jacket pocket and closed his eyes, better to imagine his wife's fragrance. Sun was wafting through a far-off window, he could almost feel it on his skin. He thought of her laughter and the way she lowered her eyes when he teased her. He remembered the mole on the nape of her neck and began to write her his weekly letter.

9
A LONG WEEKEND

Eikeboom Farm, in the Cederberg, to an arbitrary moss-frosted pool on the way to Sneeuberg Hut — round trip approximately 10 kilometres

There were four of us who arrived at Sanddrif, in the Cederberg, late one Friday evening, with just enough light left in the sky by which to pitch our tents. I mucked in with Jake, our middle son, while Sam, our eldest, pitched his borrowed igloo under a weeping willow with Skye, his girlfriend. After tent-making, I sweet-talked a group of young neighbours into sharing their wood. We built a braai, and opened beer and wine. As we stood around, admiring the oaks and yellow leaves of the nearby grey poplars, we all reached the same conclusion: we hadn't brought any camp chairs and had nowhere to chop vegetables or prepare food. As I wondered who was going to blame Dad first, our collective mood was further soured when a 50-strong group of Christians burst into a spirited delivery of 'Our God is an awesome God'. They were seated in a large circle three campsites along, and were well prepared with lamplight and microphones and amplifiers. Jake, who had received a high-Anglican education, recognised several other hymns, but the agnostics and atheists among us were none the wiser. As night fell, we realised that they seemed to be getting disturbingly high on heavenly good cheer, a sort of cosmic camaraderie. There was even some manly shouting. It took us a while to realise that they were on retreat, singing lustily to God under stars that showed no obvious evidence of His Presence. We prepared ourselves for a long weekend.

Across from our pitch on the other side of a grassed depression was a recently built prefabricated cottage, a bright bulb shining on its stoep. Beneath it was one of those all-in-one units of moulded plastic consisting of a table and two benches. We noticed that no one was at home, so Sam and Jake pounced, stealthily redeploying the unit to where it would be more useful. As they lugged the heavy table off the porch and across the dark lawn we could see them briefly silhouetted against the back wall like cartoon burglars and, watching from across the hollow, Skye and I laughed. We knew God would surely punish us for our reflex to redistribution, finding some way to expose our heathen souls. To make sure that he didn't cotton on as quickly as he might, we dumped our new find behind our raised campsite braai. Morning would render it more visible but for now we could eat and prepare our meal – sosaties, green salad and corn – in comparative invisibility, hoping that we wouldn't be bumped off our pitch because, arriving in semi-darkness, we hadn't managed to find our assigned site. After more hymns, this time led by a thick-fingered guitarist, we tucked in, although every car light that brushed over us was greeted with a little collective tremor. At about ten o'clock, the washing-up done, the singing died down. The Christians dispersed. We could see torchlights and headlamps poking about in the darkness. A couple walked up the steps to the stoep from where we had stolen their bench, searching for the front-door key. It was then that they noticed something was missing. They stood about, hands on hips, muttering; they shone their torch into the darkness and walked the length of the stoep, hoping the perpetrators would reveal themselves. Eventually they went inside and closed the door. We alternated between feeling smug and guilty. There was discussion in the morning about admitting our heinous deed and offering to take the bench back.

Of course, we didn't take it back. The occupants of the cottage left on Saturday, and the new tenants didn't know it was missing, so we continued supping with the devil. Instead we went walking, parking the car at Eikeboom, an old farm back along the Algeria Road. We noticed that there weren't many oaks left. A recent veld fire had burnt much of the bush and scrub, and we huddled the car under a single blackened old tree, a carpet of acorns at its base. Our destination was vague. I'd hoped we might traverse the valley, walking onto the tableland above before having lunch at Sneeuberg Hut, which I'd found marked on my old Forestry Department map. If feeling sufficiently perky, we might head off to the Maltese Cross afterwards, and wind our way back in a circular route. It wasn't to be. We'd overslept. Sam had mixed pancake batter back in Cape Town and we couldn't leave without breakfast. With Skye on the horizon, Sam had changed. When he was at home for the Christmas holidays and they couldn't be

together, she with her dad and stepmother on a farm outside of Plett, he'd dusted off his trainers and suddenly started
to jog because she was an avid jogger. Our phone bill sky-
rocketed. Now he was taking a blender full of pancake batter
to the Cederberg. While shopping in Rondebosch on the day
we'd driven up, I'd wondered about the purpose of the boudoir biscuits and mascarpone cheese that had found their
way into our trolley. At some point, difficult to recall exactly,
I suddenly understood. Dad's tinned-peaches-and-custard
route (one helping eaten out of the tin, probably by him) was
no longer permissible. Catering arrangements needed to be
taken to the next level. As far as the preparation and presenta-
tion of food was concerned, the Skye was clearly the limit.

As we brushed our way upwards, tiptoeing across boggy
patches and threading our way through lush, water-fuelled
growth, we started to notice groups of fantastic pink plants
growing on the island in the middle of the jeep track. They
were inverted candelabras with small pink flowers cascading
forth like a burst of tiny fireworks. We admired them and
took photographs, clambering upwards. We were now in an
area that was called Sederhoutkloof and would later walk past
Tierhok Farm and the Hoogvertoon peak. On earlier trips
to the Cederberg, during university holidays and subsequent
visits, I had been foolish enough to actually look for the
mythical cedar tree. The problem was that you can never be
sure you've actually seen one because, invariably, contrarily,
they find their way to the most obscure ledge or some diffi-
cult-to-reach crevice. Once or twice, I've thought I might
have spotted a cedar but, then again, once or twice I might

also have spotted a mermaid. I'm not sure there were ever cedars in the Cederberg, its very name being part of the perversity of the place. It might just be some homespun public-relations exercise by those wily Nieuwoudts of Dwarsrivier. Calling a region after a rare tree had a certain cachet. It was all a scam to bring wide-mouthed hicks in monster four-by-fours from the city, and a good way to increase sales of craft beer and rooibos-tea soap. Then there were the small jars of Nescafé Gold in the Dwarsrivier shop selling at R112 a pop. My bullshit detector flickered crazily, nudging into the red zone. I developed a sudden taste for Ricoffy I didn't know I had.

Yet cedars there were. In her book, *My Cederberg Story*, Olive Nieuwoudt, who lived on Kromrivier Farm for many years, recounts the tale of the original inhabitants of Garskraal (or what in time would become known as Algeria). Apparently, a ship's crew either mutinied or their ship ran aground near Lambert's Bay. Those who survived trekked inland, reaching the Olifant's River and present-day Clanwilliam. From here the party followed the Grootkloof and thrust into the mountains. They camped where they narrowed, building stone houses with reed roofs and planting gardens. They took Khoikhoi wives. They felt safe in the valley and water was abundant but their subsistence lifestyle was precarious, their supplies always meagre. When climbing out of the valley one day (in the vicinity of the present-day Middelberg hut), the men of Garskraal discovered forests of cedars. They needed to supplement their income, so they began to cut them down, believing they would always find more. 'The six feet-long blocks [of cedar wood] were loaded on a sleigh, dragged down the mountain and then taken to Tulbagh to be sold for a rijks-daler (about one shilling and sixpence),' writes Nieuwoudt. 'In later years donkeys were used to load the planks and bring them down the mountain to be loaded onto carts and taken to Clanwilliam to be sold.'

Nieuwoudt's book is full of homespun Cederberg stories, one of which is her own. Her father was a London-based merchant banker, a Dutchman of Spanish decent. He worked in the City, his family living in a beautiful old manor house on the river at Thames Ditton. Shortly after Neville Chamberlain declared war on Germany, Olive's parents decided to evacuate her and her two brothers to Cape Town. They sailed on the Union Castle mail ship, the *Cape Town Castle*, one of the last passenger liners to reach South Africa unscathed. The book shows photos of her father's wartime letters to South Africa, with drawings of plants and flowers in the margin. He stayed behind, only joining the rest of the family after the war, miraculously escaping harm when a German doodle-bug bomb plunged into their home's ample garden.

As they grew older, Olive's brothers became dedicated hikers and mountain climbers. They fell in love with the Cederberg and occasionally took her along on their adventures. During one such trip she became smitten with Rensie Nieuwoudt, the son of Wit Andries and Spuytjie of Krom-rivier. She married into a warm family but a hard life. Rensie nearly missed their wedding because it was winter and the Cederberg's rivers were in flood but finally managed to cut a way through and find his way to the church in Cape Town. Settling down, Olive was at first taken aback by the primitive hygiene of the farm kitchen, without a fridge or running water. But she prevailed, and the farm prospered, thanks in no small part to their long trips to Cape Town's markets in their squat Dodge truck. 'I sometimes went with the lorry during the summer months when it took vegetables and fruit to the old Sir Lowry Road market. We drove through the night, and although it was an exhausting journey, lasting seven hours, I always enjoyed the trip. In 1961, when the new Uitkyk Pass and the low-water bridge over the Olifant's River were built, the trip was shortened by two hours. After our children were born the entire family would accompany Rensie to the new Epping Produce Market. We usually arrived after midnight with excited children thrilled to see the lights of Cape Town. We then had to off-load our lorry of vegetables and fruit. It was usually about three o'clock by the time we arrived at my parents' house, relieved to be able to rest for what remained of the night.'

We were now walking along a road that Rensie and Olive's produce-filled truck would have frequently passed, pulling onto the tableland above. The gravel road spun gently up the kloof and I wondered if, perhaps, cartloads of cedars had once rattled down this very track, intersecting with the gravel road to the Uitkyk Pass, which tumbles towards Algeria and the gateway to Clanwilliam. Rounding a corner at our road's highest point, we stopped to drink water and Game. The children larked about and took photographs of themselves, the land falling away beneath in staggered steps. I pottered, examining the bend. Inlaid across the road was a run-off channel for rainwater. It was made of dressed sandstone and was neatly functional in a way that charmed me. I touched the warm, soft stone. There was a collection of weeds and sand sediment where the water should have run off into the abyss below and I pushed sand over the edge, clearing out a channel. As always, the act gave me a pleasure too simple to describe, something so elemental that words seem redundant. When Eikeboom was a functioning farm, people would have walked up and down this gravel track, and cedar-filled wagons would have trundled heavily down these looping roads. History was throwing us a crumb across the great void of time.

Nieuwoudt writes about the forestry workers, who sometimes referred to themselves as '*die kloof se Basters*', circling through this land, hacking out paths and firebreaks, sometimes even blasting roads. They would leave Algeria with provisions and quietly vanish, spending weeks at a time camping under the stars. It also fell to them to lay Forestry Department telephone lines – back-breaking work. They hauled creosoted telephone poles vast distances, hanging the lines, so that lookouts at remote stations on the Welbedacht, Uilsgat and Middelberg peaks could make emergency calls when they spotted summer fires. Just after Christmas 1989, one such fire all but ruined Kromrivier, causing millions of rands of damage. Nieuwoudt's book is for the most part casually matter-of-fact, with few descriptive flourishes. It moves slowly, gathering force from the accumulated descriptions of who lived where and what happened there. But a sadness trickles into the book when she describes the Kromrivier fire because, as she says, 'the farm never really recovered'. Fifty thousand hectares of snow protea, cedars and fynbos were destroyed in the blaze. More than the physical destruction it caused, the fire burnt a path through Nieuwoudt's heart.

For all its harsh charm, the Cederberg can plunge the sensitive into melancholy. Stephen Watson, the poet and scholar, spent part of the winter of 1996 at Kromrivier, an episode recorded in *A Writer's Diary*, his journal of the year. Watson loved this land, its light and silence, what he beautifully called the 'primal hours'. While here, he seemed to live on little but lentils, books and the fumes of his own unhappiness, and, after a while, the constant references to writers Joseph Brodsky and Janet Malcolm don't seem to matter as much as you suspect he intended they should. Instead of parading his erudition and angst, after a while you want Watson to do something odd or daftly human and record that in his diary. You want him to pull out a copy of *Penthouse* or detail how, serendipitously, he made a tasty meal from leftovers at the back of the fridge. If there was a mouse in the corner of his draughty cabin as he did his Walden thing, we want to know about the gentle comedy of their relationship. We want story, levity, a sprinkling of wit. We want to know, too, how he repaired his rucksack or improvised with an inconveniently snapped lace. How does his body feel when he walks; how exactly does the sun warm his back? Where is the drama and the joy? Beyond a certain point, we don't want to know about the complicated cruelties of Philip Larkin's relationships with women, or the fact that the *Cape Times* is an irredeemably lousy newspaper – we know this already. We want to know that the first thing he's going to do when he gets back home to Woodstock is put J.J.

Cale's 'Troubadour' on the turntable before shuffling a few steps across the lounge floor. Then he's going to have his first proper hot shower in months, and when he gets out he's going to get into a comfortable corduroy shirt that a woman he once loved had bought for him in Paris. It was January, and cold. They had so little money that they had to share their hot chocolate, sipping from the same large drinking bowl, discovering that their coated lips frequently came together.

* * *

Now we clambered upwards, the day hot, our pace lazy. The air was still up here on the tableland, a shimmering vault of sky opening up beyond rock and weathered sandstone like the lid of a tin can. I knew our pace was too leisurely, our intentions too indistinct. Neither Sam nor Jake were wearing caps, while Skye had wrapped herself in an impressive straw hat that flapped about her head like a wilting sunflower. Despite lashings of sunscreen lotion, the boys were going to get burnt, so I wanted to nudge the rabble towards shade and water. Sam suggested likewise, and soon we were bundu-bashing, clambering down towards where the colour of the bush deepened and the land narrowed. We aimed to find water, and water we eventually found in the form of a gentle, mossy pool, where the stream was purified by fat tufts of weeping water grass that fell from a ledge above. I was Jonah, picnicking in the mouth of a whale.

Skye and the boys found a rock behind the thin fall of water and grass, and perched upon it, cross-legged, chin raised, tips of forefinger and thumb held gracefully in front of them.

They maintained this divine pose only for as long as it took to take photos on their cellphones, before smiling big wet smiles and collapsing into hysterical laughter.

We hauled out supplies: mountain bread and Provita, tuna and mussels, cutting and slicing on a makeshift table. I opened the can with my Swiss penknife and doled out chunks of tuna mayonnaise. Sam had brought lemon to sprinkle on the mussels and salt for seasoning. We munched companionably, listening to the slow spill of the waterfall. We passed around nuts and biltong, and filled our bottles. There was life in the pools around us, squint crabs and curious frogs. One long-legged little fellow didn't seem in the slightest bit perturbed by my big toe alongside, just as long as it remained still. Everywhere were tadpoles in various stages of their life cycle. In some you could see thin legs protruding out of their tails; with others their large eyes were clearly too big for their heads. It was all peaceful and strangely theatrical, watching the dance of life in the pools at our feet. I was reminded of a snake rubbing itself out of an old skin. Everywhere we now looked, there was the same eternal chafe, profound in its matter-of-factness. You could almost feel our deepening contentment as I broke off squares of chocolate for dessert. I felt in no state to offer up an argument disputing God's existence, although I was pleased there were no hymns to break the silence.

Back at the Sanddrif campsite an hour or two later, the boudoir and mascarpone conundrum was solved. Sam was shooting out the lights – catering-wise, that is – by being the first 22-year-old to bring alfresco tiramisu to the Cederberg.

He prepared it on the stolen table, sitting on the stolen chair, while we ribbed him gently, scoffing chips and comparing our two remaining craft beers by sharing sips. We now felt part of the campsite in a way we hadn't when we arrived. There was the crazy Afrikaner guy with the long hair and button earring, his high-pitched voice travelling further than he possibly realised. His wife or girlfriend had decorated a gazebo next to their tent with fairy lights and hanging charms, as though she were about to offer the Christians a reading of the tarot or an introductory half-hour of aromatherapy. He was always yacking like a garrulous troll, while she seemed to spend the weekend in self-enforced silence, floating through her gazebo like a mermaid. On the other side of our tents was the group I'd borrowed wood from. I noticed when I replaced it that two of the young women we had passed earlier in the day in the Sederhoutkloof were doing yoga. They were cooking from a large potjie and their campsite looked Saturday-afternoon chilled. We were pretty relaxed ourselves. We'd brought kindling off the mountain and there was the fire to feed. There was dinner to prepare and the fast-falling night to admire. Charitably, and with infinite mercy, we would accommodate the Christians when they burst into song. It was no trouble at all. They had simply become part of Sanddrif's colour, like the fast-yellowing leaves on the poplars.

As I drifted off uncomfortably to sleep that night, nibbled by the cold already spreading along the banks of the river, I listened to the sounds of the campsite. The list was what I heard then and what I thought I heard, what sounds the campsite had always made and what it might have made earlier in the evening. Now drowsy and a little drunk, I suddenly didn't mind the Christian retreat because it seemed congruent with where we were. Perhaps I had mellowed and was now used to the shouting man. I could hear the unmistakable sound of tent flaps unzipping, of washed cutlery jostling on an enamel plate. I heard the rustle of bodies as they hunkered down into sleeping bags, mattresses inflated for the night. Voices came from far away and occasionally there was a creeping from the nearby bulrushes. Sometimes, fleetingly, I might almost have heard the wind scything through the oak and willow leaves nearby. There is nothing quite like the lap and lull of campsite sounds to launch you off to sleep.

The following morning the children left for Cape Town, while I stayed behind, upgrading to Orion, a nearby cottage, for a couple of nights to think and write. We played Frisbee before they left, sinking into the lush green lawn in front of the cottage where we'd stolen the bench, a tender finale to a happy weekend. Both boys had left home. Jake was in his second year at the University of Cape Town, Sam in his fourth. Lisa and I were learning to say goodbye – and welcome them back when they returned as young adults. It wasn't easy. Somehow we all slip back into the habits we once had – former personas and roles. Back home for the Christmas holidays, Sam had a bout of the grumps. He accused me of not taking him seriously, not listening with enough care. Worse still, I was slovenly and set in my ways. What was it with the green T-shirt from Mazeppa Bay? Was I going to wear it until it fell off my shoulders? The finger-pointing hurt, but he was probably right, because I was on holiday too and, besides, the pain of being a writer sometimes brought me face to face with *my* inner grump. On top of it all, I was discovering that parting with our children was fraught and painful, and every time we were reunited I was compelled to do it again. Although we had come into these mountains to honour them, to walk their roads and admire their orange peaks, I realised afterwards that we had also come to Sanddrif to say goodbye to the children we once knew. Here was the willowy, good-looking Jake, adapting to life out of the parental home; and here was cerebral Sam, reaching for Skye with tiramisu. He was beautiful, they both were, and he was no longer ours. Frisbee was a balm, it always had been. I loved the way it curled gently over the grass, shuttling between the three of us, its silence as pure as a bowed arrow. Yet it was only a vague consolation. My heart was full of noise – it always would be – sore in ways I didn't fully understand.

Thinking about it afterwards, I was reminded of that lovely scene in Richard Linklater's movie *Boyhood*, where Mason is in the midst of packing up to go to college. 'This is the worst day of my life,' sobs his mother from a corner of the lounge as he casually stows luggage in his pickup, lost in what a teacher describes earlier in the film as 'voluptuous panic'. I knew how Mason's mum felt, although in my case it was more of a long ache than a dramatic bout of tears. Feelings are never quite as neatly finished or sheer-sided as films and novels suggest. They're messier, less a clearly defined terminus than a churning voyage. Rather than coming to a clear end, they simply get overtaken by other things. Just the outline remains, the coffee-cup stain on the much-loved table of our lives. It was absolutely right that the children went off to varsity, brought their girlfriends home, ate their way through the religiously restocked fridge. The alternative – that they overstayed their welcome at home – was too horrible for either Lisa or me to contemplate. This didn't of course mean that we didn't curl up inside when it became time for them to leave again. Middle age has only something to do with creaky knees and the menopause. It's far more existential – a revolving door of goodbyes. Two years ago I stood around blank and disbelieving as my mother's coffin rolled into the crematorium fires. My sister and her family had recently breezed off to Sydney. Friends and family had fled, going on to reinvent themselves as English or Americans. Colleagues had died of cancer or heart attacks, their lives turned off as if someone had flicked a switch. I was always reaching for unsoiled words, proper words, by which to say goodbye, sort of comfortable in the knowledge that such words probably can't be found. It was a case, it sometimes seemed, of goodbyes without end. It saddened me to think that so much life – of *my life* – had simply melted away, and I was powerless to do anything about it.

When all was said and done, this was what Watson was trying to do in his diary, wasn't it: to get a better grip on the unpromising material that was his life? He thought that coming into the Cederberg might lead to a spiritual lifting of the clouds, but he seemed to sink into quicksand instead. Every so often, a bright light. The entry for 13 March 1996 concerns an article in *The New Yorker* by journalist Lawrence Weschler. The magazine had sent Weschler to The Hague to cover the Yugoslav War Crimes Tribunal and, according to Watson, the author makes the 'ingenious connection' between the Bosnian atrocities and the Vermeers hanging in the Mauritshuis in the same city. 'It's almost as if Vermeer can be seen, amidst the horrors of his age, to have been asserting or inventing the very idea of peace,' Watson quotes from the Weschler article. This, of course, is what Watson was trying to do in his diaries and poems; he was trying to hold the thin flame of his art against the gales of contemporary South Africa, blowing with greater vulgarity and carelessness with each passing year. Perhaps the solace of the Cederberg was for him the equivalent of what in Vermeer would have been the maid churning butter, or the *huisvrou* in her starched bonnet doing needlework? 'It now seemed to me,' Watson quotes Weschler, 'sitting among the Vermeers that afternoon at the Mauritshuis, that that was precisely what the Master of Delft had been about in his life's work: at a tremendously turbulent juncture in the history of his continent he had been finding – and, yes, inventing – a zone filled with peace, a small room, an intimate vision … and then breathing it out.'

'Breathing it out' is a felicitous phrase, sublime shorthand for what all artists are presumably trying to do: breath against bullets, life against death, peace against terror.

* * *

Although Watson's misery has a cloying, claustrophobic quality, he needs to be given his due. I had come into the

Cederberg partly because of him. His writing had sung the place into existence, made it more imaginatively real. Yes, on my latest reading, his diary had irritated me because he seemed to wallow in his influences and his loneliness, but there was still a spiky contrariness to the voice. Who in his right mind would write admiringly about Guy Butler? Was this a kind of ritualised academic suicide or someone with a perverse sense of humour? It was neither, because I'd read *Karoo Morning*, and I felt washed by the book, by its fidelity and the lightness of its step, its endless images of untarnished Cradock happiness. I liked it that Watson liked Albert Camus. I liked it that he got pissed off about black protest poetry in the 70s. He was nothing if not committed to remaining himself. He got huffy and mad, and I enjoyed the fact that he was honest enough to parade his dislikes, even though it meant courting disaster from the literary fashionistas. In that way, Watson and I were kindred spirits – increasingly, we just didn't care. Earn a living, honour your people and the rest is pure horseshit, as John Berger might or might not have said. Watson, as he reminded us in his diary, had been taken into these mountains by his father when he was a boy, just as I'd been taken into the Wolkberg, the Magaliesberg and the Drakensberg by my old man when I was a boy. Coming back here was an attempt to recreate the handful of images that opened Watson's youthful heart, and in one of them he recalls stumbling upon the Middelberg hut as a seven-year-old one rainy September afternoon. 'There were paper packets of tea,' he writes in the diary entry for 12 May 1996, 'coarse-ground coffee and pipe tobacco. Beside the door was a pair of Wupperthal veldskoen, the white leather uppers cut low, car-tyre soles curling; and a walking stick cut from a sapling, one end bevelled and polished by the grip of its owner's hand. On the floor of the hut, compacted of earth and dung, a bed of fresh slangbos had been crushed by sleeping bodies. Mixed in with its fragrance, was the grey smell of mutton fat.'

With passages like this, Watson redeems the diary, pushing it towards something more vivid and tactile. For us, on our pseudo-walk, what moved me was nothing more than a sandstone run-off channel cut at an angle across the neck of a road, an act of anonymous labour by forgotten men. I never knew that something so basic could be so touching. But then I never knew that having grown-up sons could be so bittersweet.

10
BLUE SQUARE IN THE MARICO

Tara Rokpa Buddhist Retreat in the Marico to the famous waterfall via the old tobacco farm and the disused irrigation canals — round trip about 10 kilometres

L ife can get pretty hairy up in the Marico. Take the battle for the Marico Eye, a seemingly endless freshwater aquifer that oozes up through black dolomitic sediment to provide a wonderland for day-trippers, scuba divers, fishermen and swimmers. The area is so subtle and ecologically sensitive that in other parts of the world none of this would be allowed but, hey, this is the Marico. It exists in a time capsule all of its own and, for decades, the Eye and the farms that surround it have been the subject of a nasty little difference of opinion. Many farms narrow as they come down to its clean, precious waters but only two farmers have any interest in clearing the reeds that circle the Eye. For the sake of fidelity to the spirit of place – and a nod in the direction of Bushveld mischief – let's call these two farmers Oom Paul and Oom Schalk. Of the two, Oom Paul was always the one, to coin a phrase, with deeper emotional waters and a greater sense of environmental pride. We will hear all about Oom Schalk in due course.

To reach Oom Paul's side of the Marico Eye, one has to first find a nondescript farm gate, which entails a right turn off the gravel section of the old Koster Road, about 20 kilometres from Koster itself. Swing through the gate and, still on gravel, head past a statuesque eucalyptus. After the stately tree – with echoes of the Deep South as you approach – is a line of six or seven weeping willows, a picnic area and ample, richly grassed land on which to park your car. As you walk towards a far smaller gate, past the bellowing yellow pump, you find your way into an enchanted kingdom, along a walkway of rudimentary planks and sheets of corrugated tin. Some of them are softened by rubber mats, some by carpet, and, after a brief, maze-like negotiation through the reeds and bulrushes, sometimes getting your shoes wet as you walk, you find your way to an open area of buoyant platforms, a diving board and a ladder. It all has a Meccano-like, let's-see-what-we-can-find-in-the-garage-like quality and is bolted and screwed together in a basic yet charming way. Oom Paul doesn't charge a cent for you to be there. Instead he invites you to plunge into enchantment. You can swim or dive or simply lounge about, peering into the black-bottomed depths through the still, glassy water at what look like endless forests of watercress and lettuce

By contrast, Oom Schalk has turned his side of the Eye into a Bushveld Disney. He built brick cottages, charges an entrance fee to weekenders and has plonked a small, flat-bottomed craft in the middle of the water. He threw in some koi fish and encouraged scuba divers to dive to the bottom. The Eye was a fountain of money. One day, long before his alterations, Oom Schalk found Oom Paul clearing reeds on the edge of the water with a shovel. The two exchanged words and, before long, both started using language the like of which they'd seldom heard themselves use before. Matters became so heated that Oom Paul found himself – with a weird, Marico-like flourish in the direction of fiction – in the holding cells of the Groot Marico Police Station. It was Christmas Day with no chance of bail. Christmas dinner and crackers containing blunt sharpeners and miniature trumpets were some way away, as were mince pies, carols and pointy hats made of crinkly paper. According to what I was told by Egbert van Bart at the Groot Marico Visitors' Information Centre, a man with a splendid beard that gives him a certain Herman Bosman-like cachet, 'Friends had to bring Oom Paul socks and clean underwear.'

Oom Paul's episode in jail accounts for why, if you visit the Eye today, you will find a barbed-wire fence running from bank to bank across the water. The fence has suspended sticks and planks hanging vertically across it at regular intervals and, at a pinch, it looks like a musical score annotated by some Bushveld Mozart. It is rumoured that if you swim under or through the fence and trespass you are likely to get shot, although Oom Paul is now in his 80s and is unlikely to don his baggies to go in for a spot of wild swimming, knowing he might take a bullet for his troubles. Oom Schalk is an absent owner anyway. He has entrusted the Disney side of the operation to a manager who seems only too happy to keep the coins and dimes rolling. In other parts of the world, the Eye would be fenced off; the walkways would be made of polished steel, the carpets along them of thick rubber. There would be parking lots and hefty entrance fees and guided tours by trained ecologists. It is the ecology of the place that is most interesting, after all. Crabs, the most sensitive of species, live here, as do otters. You can see the faded pink and white of freshwater crab shells everywhere and you can see shell in the abundant droppings scattered on the carpet and occasional cushions that Oom Paul has helpfully put out for visitors. Best of all, the Eye's mysteriously deep waters are home to a species of freshwater eel. The eels migrate from here, the fairy-tale headwaters of the Marico River, northwards to the Crocodile River. In time, the Crocodile flows into the Limpopo, and the Limpopo fans sluggishly into the Indian Ocean. Once the eels reach the ocean they still have thousands of kilometres to swim to the west coast of Madagascar, where they spawn. In time, they do the journey in reverse, eventually returning to the soft, translucent water of the Eye, where the stems of a thousand water lilies dance upward in search of sunlight.

The spat between Oom Schalk and Oom Paul was a prelude to a larger and potentially far more damaging stand-off in the area between local environmentalists and traditional leaders on the one hand, and multinational mining houses, like De Beers, on the other. Since 2006 there have been six applications for prospecting licences and, although none has been granted, environmentalists in the Marico are of the view that their 10-year battle might be reaching its endgame. At a recent public meeting to discuss the issue, a group of local hotheads warned that there could be 'no guarantee' that farm murders wouldn't increase in the area should the De Beers application be rejected, a statement that was in no way challenged by those De Beers officials present. For many, the area, with its sumptuous sunsets and mellow talk of moon shadow, is a haven only three hours' drive from Gauteng. For the mining houses and their representatives, however, this is an area of unprecedented mineral richness. De Beers believe that diamonds will be found in the kimberlite rock and this will mean massive open-cast mines, probably bringing fewer jobs and less direct investment than some in the community would like to believe. There are fears that should a licence be granted, then even if diamonds aren't found, minerals of comparative value will be. 'With kimberlite, the prospectors' drills go from 380 metres to 600 metres deep. That's penetrating the water table and that's dangerous,' said a member of the local anti-mining lobby, who declined to be named.

When my wife and I walked in the area, we walked mainly on the land of the Tara Rokpa Buddhist Retreat, about 10 kilometres from the Marico Eye. For some of the way we walked along a minor tributary of the Marico that falls just outside of the blue square of potential prospecting you frequently come to see on both the environmentalists' and the De Beers maps. It was a lovely walk in a landscape that seemed to be just a little sadder and more whimsical than usual. Indeed, it might even have had something of that 'sweet sadness' that Herman Charles Bosman refers to in 'Marico Revisited'; 'There is the gentle melancholy of the twilight, dark eyes in faces upturned in a trancelike pallor. And fragrances. And thoughts like soft rain falling on old tomb-stones.'

Putting aside Bosman's more florid excesses for the moment, it was noticeable from talking to people like Pippa Cope of the Buddhist retreat, and keeping one's eyes and ears open, that here was a tough, bone-hard landscape, not amenable to very much, whether it be love or fertiliser. Cattle rustling across what was then the Bechuanaland border was ubiquitous, with stolen cattle being herded into the difficult-to-find Agterkloof to wait for the inevitable search parties to pass by. The Boer War was devastating. The men galloped gallantly off on commando, leaving the women and children behind. As the war progressed and the slippery Boers proved more and more elusive, Lord Kitchener's scorched-earth strategy blackened the veld. Farms and farm buildings were torched by the British, and the women and children were rounded up and put in concentration camps like the one in Mafeking. Living conditions were deplorable and unsanitary. Those who survived nursed a deep sense of grievance and injustice against the British, sometimes amounting to hatred. When normality resumed after the war, the Boer farmers simply did it all again, trying to wring a living out of this mutely indifferent, strangely captivating but often unprepossessing land.

A stone's throw away from Tara Rokpa's open-air communal eating area at the beginning of our walk, we peered into empty, kikuyu-swamped ponds where the previous owner had tried to farm fish. After that we walked alongside an irrigation canal, since collapsed, sometimes full of soft leaves, sometimes tantalisingly clear in outline. Within minutes, as we followed Pippa and her whippet-like dog, we stumbled across a road and onto an old farm. She told us that the family, who live on the West Rand, come back to the area only once a year – to celebrate what used to be Geloftedag, or the Day of the Vow. The farmhouse walls were made of unfired mud bricks, and there was an outside privy and a shed up on the hill. A bread-making oven stood on the property, and Lisa and I were intrigued by a garage containing two dusty ox-wagons, one painted red and green. Next to the garage, at ground level, were two slate-covered pits, possibly used for storing tobacco and, alongside, what we took to be a primitive curing shed, perhaps a smoking shed for freshly killed meat – we were undecided. 'It took a span of 18 oxen two days to transport a wagonload of tobacco from here across the hills and into Groot Marico,' Pippa told us. 'There was a short-lived tobacco boom in this part of the Transvaal and the farmers were always trying their luck on new things because farming was so marginal.'

As we bashed up the gentle hill behind the farm, looking out for round yellow route markers, I reflected on what we'd just seen. One of the oxwagon wheels was made of seven slightly bent pieces of hardwood laid head to tip and surrounded by an upper and a lower steel rim. The brakes were similarly rudimentary, made from blocks of what looked like ironwood – and the base or floor above the wheels looked cradle-like, deeper in the middle and rising to its winged tips. Being a less-than-adept carpenter, I was in awe of it all, although not so taken that I didn't realise that it would make for one very uncomfortable ride. It would have surely been better to walk. I couldn't readily imagine what sleeping on the floor of an oxwagon was like. If it was safe it would have been better to nod off in the veld, as Oom Schalk Lourens had done in Bosman's 'In the Withaak's Shade', his short story about Bushveld cunning and bullshit.

At the top of the rise we followed the meanders of the upper contour. Beneath us to our left was a cattle-splashed valley, across to our right were gently disappearing hills sliced by a gravel road that was almost black – the same colour as the earth at the bottom of the Eye. We blundered on, a little uncomfortably. Baboons had bent some of the yellow marker discs in half and sometimes they had simply vanished from the path they were meant to lead us along. A veld fire had swept along this ridge recently. You could see the felled aloes and blackened bushes and fire-licked proteas. With the fire and ash, though, was new life, a fresh sprouting of grass and greenery. Looking about, you sensed that the fire hadn't rolled across this landscape in a destructive, all-consuming ball; rather it had brushed across the grass and kissed the trees with flame, allowing for regeneration and rebirth. There was life here, much of it healthy, and although the route was broken at times and a little higgledy-piggledy, the two of us ploughed on along the sometimes phantom track. We bashed through a detour, down into a section of indigenous forest on the western slope of the tableland, and continued tracking the contour as it flowed away from us in a roughly south-westerly direction. After another 20 minutes of walking we saw a green sign to the waterfall nailed to a tree. The route dropped us quickly into a gulley, now dry, but during a downpour it would quickly become wet and dangerous. It was a scramble, sometimes best negotiated on your bum. After about 10 or 15 minutes, we creaked our way to the valley floor, knees and ankles slightly worse for wear. The path forked just beyond the base of a green, mossy stump, and before long we were peeling naartjies at the foot of a terraced waterfall, its water collecting in a brown, orange-tinged pool at our feet.

After a pit stop – for me to jot down notes while Lisa took photos, both of us admiring the ferns and delicate folds of greenery on the surrounding walls – we turned our back on the waterfall. Before long I spotted the remnants of the canal we'd seen at the beginning of the walk as Pippa and her dog, Chokyi, had put us on the overgrown pathway. I noticed that the canal ran roughly parallel to the river – no doubt once a channel for irrigating the farmland at the base of the valley. Before long the path had become a jeep track. Shortly after that we burst free of the indigenous bush and headed towards open pastureland, skipping our way through a group of passive, wide-eyed cows. We noticed a collapsed windmill, lolling on its side, like some stricken creature from Mars out of H.G. Wells's *The War of the Worlds*. Tucking into our sandwiches a little later, I discovered the disused canal again. It had filled with weeds and leaves; at some points it had lost its shape, collapsing. Sometimes it was choked, sometimes almost impossible to divine. Still, it appealed to the boy in me. It was probably built in the 1920s or 30s, when this land was still a promise, irrigating the cabbage fields, the lucerne, perhaps the tobacco, with the water running into a little culvert or weir at the back of the farmhouse. I realised in my reveries that you could trace the canal's line by the vegetation that had grown around it and along its banks. The water was now gone but trees remained, ghosts and shadows of what once was.

Pippa mentioned later that the old farmers had built a dam further down the valley. It didn't withstand its first flood. The dam wall was brushed aside as if by a runaway loco-motive, and the rubble deposited high on the banks, far down-stream. She asked if we'd noticed the remnants of the wall, and we admitted we hadn't, although we had spent a few dis-consolate minutes visiting the Oberholzer family graveyard perched on a cutting above the wagon road. There were about 25 graves in all, many for babies and children. Hester Petronella Oberholzer, for example, only lived to see the month of May – no more. Eighteen months later, young Maria Elizabeth Adriana Oberholzer didn't see her second week, dying in late 1933, *'Hier rus ons dogtertjie'* read the plaintive words on her gravestone. A few headstone inscrip-tions – made of a slightly damp, clay-like sandstone – were hand-carved. Long words weren't always elegantly dealt with, and one's eye strained to make out the hidden letters, only to find them snapped off mid-sentence when the scribe ran out of space. The rudimentary carvings – flowers and aloes – in the gravestones' margins only added to the heaviness of the experience. Later one of Pippa's stories cast a further shadow. She explained how a row had broken out when she and others had wanted to include graves for some black deceased in an all-white farm graveyard on the Buddhist retreat's land. Naturally, it was a spat prefigured in Bosman, although in this case there was no yellow dog to mooch over mixed bones, no droll authorial voice to remind us of the appropriate clichés about death being the great leveller.

Somewhere along here we held hands like young lovers until it became impossible to continue walking side by side. It was good to be outdoors in the plump autumn sunshine, life-blessed and strong. We left the irrigation canal before long and sauntered into the afternoon, happy in speechless grace. Later, having fallen asleep on the grass at the Buddhist retreat, we drifted to the Eye, admiring its soft waters, trying not to be too judgemental about the raucous sounds of the weekenders on Oom Schalk's side of the barbed-wire fence. We were told that the Eye – in effect, a merry natural pump – flushed water from just beyond the Koster Road northwards through the town of Groot Marico, where Egbert van Bart told us his marvellously wry stories at the information centre as he stroked his beard at just the right time. When looked at in three dimensions the Eye formed part of a raised, north-facing plateau, funnelling water towards the Marico Bushveld Dam and past Koffiekraal, Brakkuil, Uitkyk and Pachsdraai. The Madikwe Game Reserve gets it water from the Eye and we were told that the Tswasa Weir, further up the river, provides Gaborone with some of its drinking water. Matters weren't perfect along the Marico's banks but land restitution had worked up to a point, with new black landowners renting their farms back to white managers. Tobacco and vegetables, like tomato, cabbage and mielies, were grown on land adjacent to the river. The traditional chiefs, or kgosis, were generally opposed to the applications for a mining licence. Environmentalists estimate that the Eye provides about 100 000 people with fresh water, most of them nominally under the traditional leaders' control. The kgosis know that mining will tamper with the water table and possibly damage the aquifer. 'We are an ignorant people, not well educated,' one of the chiefs is reputed to have said, 'but we are a wise people. Mining is not a good idea.' It's a quote echoed in Bosman, where he writes about a Bechuana chief who once visited former King George V at Buckingham Palace. When asked what the two men talked about, the chief replied archly: 'We kings know what to discuss.' So, in true Marico style, fact cleaves to fiction. There is wisdom along the banks of the Marico; there is perhaps even wisdom available for those who drink the Marico Eye's plentiful and soft waters.

* * *

For all his prescience and understanding, Bosman didn't foresee that a stout Tibetan Buddhist called Akong Rinpoche would identify land roughly between the N4 and the brick-red road between Koster and Zeerust as the site for a Buddhist retreat and, later, if money allowed, a temple. In 1959 Rinpoche was part of a group of 300 Buddhist monks and converts who fled to India from Chinese persecution in Tibet. It was a walk through ice and fire because those who didn't perish on the trek (or weren't butchered by Chinese bullets) struggled in India, according to Cope, unable to deal with the clammy heat and strange food. Of the original 300 who had started the great walk to freedom, only 13 members of the group survived.

After several years struggling in an Indian refugee camp, Rinpoche and two fellow monks were able to flee to England, one of them receiving a place at Oxford. Rinpoche became an orderly at an Oxford hospital, supporting all three and, over time, they converted an unused hunting lodge in rural Dumfrieshire into a Buddhist retreat – Britain's first. The three couldn't agree on matters spiritual or practical, however, and they separated, leaving Rinpoche in charge of the retreat. He renamed the former lodge Samye Ling and, having always been a homely and practical man, set about making changes and improvements.

'In the early days, one resident recalls, he would repair bed sheets and blankets with a hand-operated sewing machine, clear blocked drains and make sure nothing was wasted,' a section culled from his obituary in *The Guardian* tells us.

Akong Rinpoche visited South Africa for the first time in 1982 and Cope met him on many occasions. He was not, she reported, a man of many words, although he was decisive and strangely alluring, possessed of a certain thick-set gravitas: 'He would walk around the property and across the grass, often murmuring in Tibetan,' she said. 'On one occasion he pulled a sling from his belt and slung small stones in the four cardinal directions. Once, at breakfast, he announced: "We're going to buy land this morning", and within a month we'd bought three farms, although money was always an issue and we were never quite sure of where to find it or how we were going to finance some of these buys. His saying was "money will come from where it is when needed". He was very sensitive to issues around the environment. He knew the land was mineral-rich and said fresh air and clean water would one day become rare resources and foretold they would become an issue in the future. In that respect, he was very wise.'

On one of his visits to Tara Rokpa, Rinpoche ventured behind the communal eating area and kitchen onto a button of land with a natural aspect northward, facing in the direction of the infamous blue square. He buried offerings and holy charms in four pits, conforming to the four points of the compass, each pit a metre deep, calling the site 'Temple Hill'. Each pit contains placatory offerings for man's destruction of the environment, offerings whose worth and power will become clearer in the months and years to come. It is, as Bosman might have put it, a queer situation. Tibetan holy men are not common in these parts, less common, say, than *rooineks* and tax collectors, less common, even, than the motor coach from Zeerust, to use Bosman's phrase, which is not, in fact, very common nowadays at all. To think that a Buddhist foresaw all these troubles and now finds himself in unlikely virtual alliance with some of the local landowners and lefties, not to mention many of the kgosis further north, is a matter worthy of long and serious contemplation. There are other interested parties. Early in 2016 a local NGO calling itself the African Pride Nature Conservation Association was formed in Reboile, the township adjacent to Groot Marico. At present they are only 18 strong but the association is full of brassy, smart youngsters who know that the area's water and natural heritage demand constant vigil and, if they do not keep, well, an eye open, it will be whisked from their grasp. Despite the opposition, the soul-destroying work of canvassing, collecting signatures and conveying information (not everyone has email in these parts and the cellphone signal is erratic), activists admit that their best chance might be if the area is turned into a conservancy. The application has been supported by the North West Parks and Tourism Board, I've been told, but it is not clear which way the political water is flowing. People in these parts are *vrot* with worry. The threat that farm murders will increase if a licence isn't granted has left an unpleasant aftertaste, and people are reluctant to be quoted, return phone calls and give their names for fear of exposure or recrimination. Here in the Marico the messy and frightening business of living in contemporary South Africa has trumped anything the famed storytellers of the far west have come up with so far, although it has provided one small hidden advantage: it has turned some members of the community into savvy environmental activists – a lobby of eye specialists, you might say.

11

THE SANDALLED SPECTRE – A WILL-O'-THE-WISP CALLED GANDHI

Museum Africa, Newtown, to the Hindu
Crematorium via the Hamidia Mosque – about
2.5 kilometres

Johannesburg history is a curiosity shop stuffed with remarkable figures and shimmering facts. One of the boom town's first two recorded deaths was from typhoid. The other, with a wink in the direction of dark comedy, records a man who fell down a mineshaft. The city's grave-yards couldn't grow quickly enough. First was the cemetery at Diagonal Street; then, further north and west, one in Braamfontein. After that came the Brixton graveyard, today almost a forest, with its own graceful bandstand, but in those days large enough to house never-ending waves of the dead. Tucked away in a corner of the Brixton Ceme-tery is the Hindu Crematorium, a national monument and the first brick-built crematorium in the southern hemi-sphere. Wood-fired and built of varnished purple brick, it is served by a fluted chimney attached to the oven, the entire complex surrounded by a shapely red-and-pink wall. Campaigned for by Gandhi and designed by Kallenbach, the need for it arose because in Johannesburg's early years there was nowhere for Hindus to be cremated. Some members of the Hindu population lived in the so-called Coolie Location, behind the present-day Museum Africa, where my father and I started our Gandhi walk.

In 1904, the same year as the Modderfontein tragedy, the location was razed, the city's response to a plague and typhoid epidemic. Without a crematorium, the Hindus who died in the location (or in a makeshift hospital close to the flour mill of today) were presumably burnt in the veld, perhaps on a ghat on the Klip River. Imagine, if you will, a field of pyres at twilight, on the town limits. The sun is dipping in the west. Oxwagons used to transport the dead are trundling across the hills. Scattered groups of mourners observe the fires, mumbling incantations. The crows bounce up and down, or argue in the air, a demented chorus.

Gandhi's journeys have a wisp-like charm. He flows through the South African imagination like a sprite, forever enterprising, always busy. His are the politics and poetics of restlessness, a prickly discontent. There is always a journey, often a walk or a march. Take the famous train ride from Durban to Johannesburg where he was evicted from a first-class carriage at Pietermaritzburg and forced to spend the night in the station waiting room. Take his moonlit walks from Tolstoy Farm to his legal chambers in Johannesburg (the record for which was four hours, 18 minutes), or the long marches across the Natal border and into Volksrust in the then Transvaal, with thousands of protesting Indian coal miners. Here was an inveterate, light-footed walker, someone who struggled to keep still. 'Initially, because Johannesburg's horse-drawn trams were reserved for whites (then known as 'Europeans') only, Gandhi felt obliged to walk between home and office,' Eric Itzkin reminds us in *Gandhi's Johannesburg*. 'When electric trams began running in February 1906 they, too, were generally reserved "For Europeans". While living in Troyeville he walked the six kilometres to and from his office. During his stay in Bellevue East, he walked still further between home and office, both ways. Later, while living in the far-flung suburb of Orchards with his friend Hermann Kallenbach, both men walked ten kilometres to their offices in town, even though Kallenbach could ride on the trams. But this pales in comparison to the thirty-five kilometre journey made by Gandhi and his followers from their settlement on Tolstoy Farm.'

While Gandhi's sandalled foot made hardly a print, my father and I were tiresome plodders, heading heavily west down Lilian Ngoyi (formerly Bree) Street from the Museum Africa parking lot one crisp Saturday morning. My dad is 79 and not the most energetic of walkers, but I'd invited him along because he loves old Johannesburg in a soulful, deeply magnanimous way. Like many of his generation, he grew up in Yeoville and Berea. He attended Wits in the 1950s and is a sort of living encyclopaedia of the city. He's written books about Joburg and its founding fathers, and when I was growing up was always on hand to pull facts and stories like rabbits from hats. It was he who told me that Kensington Ridge was the southernmost continental divide, meaning that if rain fell slightly south of the apex of the ridge, it ultimately wound its way into the Atlantic Ocean via the Natalspruit,

Klip, Vaal and Orange. If, however, rain fell slightly to the north of the ridge, the water found its way into the Jukskei, the Crocodile and the Limpopo, eventually disgorging into the Indian Ocean. The story held me spellbound. I love the idea of the continental tipping point, and the, ahem, impossibly fine scales of natural justice.

As far as our ramble was concerned, Dad had been practising for days, I found out later, walking up and down the pathways of his retirement home in a regime of gentle septuagenarian training. Training or not, his pace wasn't quite swift enough for me. I often found myself walking ahead only to stop in mild irritation when I found he wasn't on my shoulder. I'd be talking as we crossed, say, Henry Nxumalo Street, and find that he wasn't with me. It meant I would either have to wait or go back, or go forward and then wait. We made for a bad couple, an odd sight as we inched down Lilian Ngoyi Street in a dark and slightly comic little cloud.

As we walked I noticed auto-repair shops and traders selling industrial-sized plastic bottles full of detergent, fabric softener and washing-up liquid. An old warehouse on the northern side of the street was being converted into a pizzeria, and a garage we passed was clearly being dolled up with new brick paving and features. We turned off Lilian Ngoyi, through the happy grime, the misaligned paving stones and the litter, heading for the Hamidia Mosque, which was closed. There was a monument outside, consisting of a three-legged cooking pot mounted on a plinth. The pot was driven by turning a handle and if you looked through the vertical slits in the pot as it circled at the right speed, you could see copies of old-fashioned pass books. It was Gandhi and approximately 3 000 other demonstrators who, in August 1908, had taken exception to these enforced pass books. 'The huge bonfire, lit in a cauldron [outside of the mosque], marked the first burning of passes in South Africa, and the beginning of satyagraha, or passive resistance campaign,' read the caption beneath.

A middling lawyer who reinvented himself as a fearless social reformer, Gandhi was just one of many in Joburg's passing parade. Another was Luscombe Searelle, impresario and shape-shifter, whose fascinating story is recorded in an exhibition in Museum Africa, now receding behind our backs. Born in Devon, shipped while young to Christchurch in New Zealand, and taking his new Christian name – he was born Isaac Israel – from the name of a small South Australian town, Searelle spotted a commercial opportunity on the goldfields of the Rand in the late 1880s. As South Africa's first Peter Toerien, however, he faced certain challenges. He needed, for instance, to ship a stage, equipment and players from Australia to Durban. From there, his theatre, replete with boxes and a bar, was transported by railway to Ladysmith – the end of the line. Onward the troupe and their props continued by oxwagon to the town of tents. 'The journey for his prefabricated wood and iron theatre took all of a week,' a caption in Museum Africa reminds us, noting helpfully that Searelle's theatre, Johannesburg's first, was officially opened on 4 May 1887.

Searelle and his wife, the renowned opera singer Blanche Fenton, didn't dumb down for the sake of the rowdy masses.

Their first performance at the Theatre Royal was the opera *Maritana*, followed by *The Bohemian Girl*. They didn't seem to mind that the audience for their first shows was made up of raucous diggers, whores, pickpockets, mountebanks and filibusterers, a casual gunman or two – they were evangelists for higher things. After the operas came Shakespeare and, in 1891, former opera star and actress Genevieve Ward was enticed to Johannesburg. In 11 weeks she steamed through 16 plays, including *Othello*, *Hamlet* and *The Merchant of Venice*. Culture-starved patrons couldn't get enough.

Searelle needed to bankroll each performance, sell tickets, do promotional work and advertising, and keep a keen eye on the punters, lest they fell out of their seats or whistled too loudly at the female lead. They were known to get uppity if the national anthem wasn't played before each performance, hurling chairs into the air and running amok. Despite Searelle's civilising mission, this was still a one-theatre town. Diggers were unused to spirited conversation, culture and reasoned debate. If they didn't like something, they'd punch you in the mug or call you outside and challenge you to a duel. The catcalls received by Charles du Val, one of Searelle's early male leads, were nothing compared with what audiences were capable of when inflamed. Indeed, several early South African theatres were burnt to the ground. Patrons' tempers ran decidedly hot.

Volumes of traffic around the Oriental Plaza, which we approached after looking at the monument outside the mosque, were thin and irregular. It was early morning and the masses of Saturday shoppers had yet to arrive. I noticed a woman cutting a coil of steel wool into more manageable – therefore saleable – sizes, as we headed up towards the bridge over the westward-nudging train tracks, past shadowy shop-fronts and still-closed concerns: Haroun Bulbulia, optometrist; Radio Islam; India Star tailors. As we crossed the bridge, Dad recalled his Christmas-holiday train trips to Cape Town as a boy. Looking down at the tracks, heading out to Mayfair and Langlaagte, he spoke of anxious excitement. He would already be in the carriage, he said, waiting for his parents to say goodbye to each other – his father stayed behind for work and would join them later – utterly convinced that his mother would miss the train. Then the five-minute whistle and the first heavy tug from the engines. Once they were moving, he could relax and admire the view. He would spend a month in Camps Bay with friends and relatives, enjoying the Camps Bay Rotunda (first a skating rink, then a ballroom), the endless summer evenings and swimming in the tidal pools. Elizabeth McNally, a girlfriend of his, lived in Camps Bay. He remembered the two of them catching a bus to the movies at The Odeon in town, swaying above Clifton, and a New Year's Eve dance at the Rotunda. He talked about the holidays wistfully. 'It was so different then,' he said. 'You were completely safe.'

After easing over the bridge, we turned northwards at the next major intersection, inching up Krause Street, past Phineas McIntosh Park, which was obscured behind buildings to our left. Fritz Krause was an early Joburg wunderkind. He was educated at Grey College, and the universities of Amsterdam and Cambridge. His legal roles were many, including Chief Prosecutor for the Witwatersrand, but he is more famous for handing a relatively intact and undamaged Johannesburg over to Lord Roberts's advancing forces during the Anglo-Boer War. It was not a popular decision because members of the Volksraad wanted the mines wrecked and the city destroyed. Roberts was to be greeted with fire and rubble. As newly appointed Special Military Commandant for the Witwatersrand, Krause demurred, and Roberts's troops filed into a largely unharmed, silent city. There was something Olympian about Krause. He was broad-minded and tolerant, strangely easy-going for a man of his times. He disagreed with Jan Smuts over Joburg's early prostitution issue, arguing liberally that men outnumbered women by vast numbers, so they were always going to drink, gamble and whore. Smuts, prickly and disapproving, couldn't agree. The two locked horns like bull elephants. Others found Krause's high-mindedness similarly irksome. Paul Kruger and Louis Botha wanted the gold mines destroyed before Roberts arrived with his sun-burnt khaki legions. Krause refused, and so they charged him, although the sanction was short-lived and soon forgiven.

Further along Krause Street was Task Academy, a boarding school, and its playing fields. We chatted to a young man through the bars of the closed school gate. He was fresh in from KwaZulu-Natal, he told us, having started his first term at the school a month before. Dad asked him about the boarding-school grub and his subject choices, as I gazed beyond his shoulder to what looked like stables fringed by a faraway sward of grass. Dad stayed on the Task Academy side of the road, while the boy resumed what looked like a chilled kick-around where even the ball gave the impression of being bored. While Dad lingered, I crossed to read a mosaic-fringed plaque commemorating Fietas on the other side of the road. The memorial was dusty but undamaged. It told that this land had started out as the Malay Location in 1893 and was formally established as Pageview in 1943. In the 60s and 70s it was flattened by apartheid's bulldozers in an act of callous spite. Pageview families, having lost their homes and their suburb, were parcelled off to Eldorado Park and Lenasia, and it now stands sadly, a scene of vacant, litter-strewn lots and drab duplexes. Every car, we noticed, was customised, every tyre fat. An old *breker* with slicked-back yellowing hair, passed us by, clutching his Saturday-morning copy of *The Citizen*. My notes record that I found only one sentence of the memorial caption interesting, presumably because it highlighted the difference between what was and what currently seems to be the case: 'It was a place of backyards and alleyways, mosques and churches, bioscopes, shebeens, corner cafés and the famous 14th Street bazaar.'

Gandhi might have been the city's first activist, and Searelle its first man of the theatre, but there were other firsts besides. Johannesburg's first barber shop and shaving saloon (next to the Golden Mortar Dispensary) was opened in 1887 at 58 Commissioner Street, within walking distance of Searelle's Theatre Royal, for instance. The shaving saloon was, in turn, a stone's throw away from the town's first butchery, Morkel's Butchers, on the corner of Bree Street and Marshall Square, not far from where we'd started our walk. Rudimentary refrigeration hadn't come to the Rand by 1886 because an old black-and-white photo in Museum Africa shows the Morkels and their knifemen surrounded by meat carcasses on three sides. There are even carcasses hanging from the ceiling, with a table of offal and tripe standing solidly in the foreground. Buying meat wouldn't have been an undertaking for the faint-hearted.

The first building with a lift (the Barbican) became operational in 1897; the first horse-drawn tram trundled down the dusty streets in 1891; and the first electronic tram came 15 years later, in 1906. The first woman to register as a licensed driver was in 1904. 'By 1913 there were four registered female drivers, with the figure mounting to eight in 1914 and 24 by 1915. The first black female driver was given her licence in 1929,' my notes tell me. The first African-language newspaper was printed in 1910, a singular achievement in a culture not renowned for progressive politics or open-mindedness. The first traffic light was erected 17 years later, in March 1927, at the intersection of Rissik and President streets, a gift from film tycoon, Isidore Schlesinger. 'It caused a sensation as people flocked to see Jo'burg's first robot. The light, however, was short-lived,' remarks a caption drolly, 'taken out by a careless motorist.'

We waited for *our* light to turn green and walked slowly through the arch of the Brixton Cemetery. It was a world of trees – Chinese elms, pride of India, London planes, as well as cedars and pines – stretching as far as they eye could see. A little further along was the main entrance, red-brick, with a board helpfully detailing the cemetery's prices. Cremations

(R700) were far more expensive than exhumations (R211), which seemed fair enough, while the fee for cremations for those over 120 kilograms weighed in at a hefty, and perturbingly arbitrary, R1 053. Scanning the list, my eye snagged on anatomy material (or, as the board had it, 'anatony material'), the price for which was R527 per 100 kilograms. I found myself wondering what anatomy material consisted of – a sort of mix 'n' match of limbs and organs? How was the price list created? I wondered. Did some city official (the Brixton Cemetery fell under the auspices of Parks and Recreation) make this kind of thing up as he or she went along, possibly after teatime on a slow Thursday? So, for example, where did the '7' come from exactly? Had they never heard of rounding up or rounding down? I wasn't used to seeing three-digit numbers finishing on seven or one – or three for that matter. And was this Parks *or* Recreation, or maybe a chummy working group consisting of both? I guessed it was Parks because you couldn't really entrust crematorium prices to Recreation – it didn't seem, well, metaphysically right. And, anyway, there was a certain linguistic congruence, a sort of fit, wasn't there, if you left all this odd-number manipulation to Parks.

You came to the Brixton Cemetery to be *parked*, after all.

This all came to me later, of course. As we plodded along I was surprisingly empty-headed, irritated by the fact my camera's memory stick had somehow frozen and I couldn't get it to work. As we walked, we noticed a couple of security guards, neatly dressed, eternally bored. I assumed they were on the graveyard shift.

One of them was sitting with his back resting on a band-stand pillar. His body language suggested that he wanted to avoid us, to be left alone to his vaguely illicit dealings. Maybe he was embarrassed. It looked as if he might be quietly brewing a pot of tea.

The security personnel seemed to live in great utopian harmony with the *bergies* and those living rough, who occasionally revealed themselves as fleeting presences away in the bushes. We trundled on, admiring the arbour, noticing the graves. Some were in good condition; some had been vandalised; some were slowly disappearing. There seemed to be no obvious pattern except for my vague feeling that this might become, given time – and Parks and Recreation's encouragement – an informal settlement. Where was the dividing line, I wondered? And was an informal settlement not a form of graveyard, after all? Perhaps it were for the best if they got together and pooled their resources.

It wasn't long before we reached the Hindu Crematorium, the end of our walk. It was early on a Saturday morning, and the gates were locked, the dogs behind them barking sullenly and without conviction. My mother had been cremated here one terrible winter morning just under two years ago. I was blank now and pretty much blank then, guilty afterwards that I hadn't had the sense of occasion to say a few words or bring along a poem to read after her coffin slid into the fires. This is the problem with families of atheists and agnostics. They have no scaffolding on which to hang their pain, no hymns or prayer books, no ritual, no convention. They stand around, useless, benumbed by the occasion, and then go out and have a meal, each in their own way trying to come to terms with their bright and not-so-bright memories, what they do and do not feel.

My mother had a lovely eye, a way with earrings and scarves and bric-a-brac and furniture. She loved her garden and a drink of wine, soap operas and a good tune. She adored the Royal Family, about whom she could be disturbingly irrational. She wrote fine letters, was intellectually self-deprecating in ways that infuriated me, and made meals of great tastiness and thrift, with just enough in the pot for meagre seconds. She didn't come from poverty but her father, a Uitenhage policeman and an alcoholic (in that order), had little left for luxuries. Her parents' relationship wasn't good and after Mom matriculated from Collegiate in the Eastern Cape she fled. She became a nurse and experienced some of the happiest days of her life. She jolled with girlfriends and dated and gossiped and went on holidays to Margate. I have photographs and they show four innocent young women having fun. I once probed her about her relationship with her parents and asked one or two questions too many. Before I could stop myself – this was the period of my life when I was determined to find out about things I didn't know – she was crying. I felt dreadful and relapsed into my customary role as the dutiful eldest son, making her laugh and clearing away the dishes.

About seven months before her death she fell and fractured her shoulder while getting into the bath. The injury was slow to heal. We didn't realise it at the time but there was probably some spiritual wear and tear because she had been battling with a dotty heart for years. The specialists were so exasperated they made gentle fun of it ('You're a medical mystery, Mrs Alfred!') and the phrase became a standing family joke. She'd worn a pacemaker for as long as we could remember and we blithely assumed that this would go on pretty much forever. Of course, we also knew that it probably wouldn't – a feeling that was sharpened when she had a stroke a couple of months after her accident getting into the bath. The stroke was cruel. Mom lost the ability to speak and although she wasn't paralysed, her walking became slow and ponderous. Not long after eventually being discharged, she contracted a gall-bladder infection. Her return to hospital (this time one closer to home) overlapped with my parents' house being put up for sale. They had lived on the bluff of a koppie at the bottom of a Kensington cul-de-sac for years and although the views of the sky and Bez Valley in autumn were majestic, they were exposed to sortie after jolly sortie of crime by local desperados. In what must have been some kind of Kensington first, the gang even managed to pull the geyser through their cottage roof, whereupon I exercised my prerogative as son and insisted they put their beautiful old house on the market. It was snapped up quicker than Dad thought. Mom's discharge from hospital after her gall bladder had cleared up coincided with their move to a small place in a retirement village opposite Queens High School, in Bez Valley. As what remained of their belongings – those that hadn't been sold or given away – were being packed up, the hospital called. I went off to collect Mom and brought her straight home. The plan was for the folks to stay in our cottage but I saw how creaky and breathless she was, and commandeered her into Jake's room, the shorter walk. She seemed to be recovering slowly when they moved in to their new place two weeks later and we were hopeful that she would see spring. By now it was the height of winter. Frost had rampaged across the lawns and, despite heaters and electric blankets, they were cold. I baked an orange cake for her birthday, which she picked at politely. Within two days she was dead, a heart attack felling her as she returned to bed one night after visiting the bathroom.

My wife and I talked about it during the final dusty stages of our Tara Rokpa Centre walk. Her view was that Mom – who had been a nurse and a psychiatric nurse, with experience of death – had decided to die. She knew herself well enough to stop eating and refuse her medication. She was brave and unsentimental to the last, although it pained us all to think that she never had the opportunity to wave her beloved Collingwood Street house goodbye.

Dad was tired after our walk and I found a place to sit down. We opened foil-wrapped chicken mayonnaise sarmies and I cracked open a beer, pouring it into two tin cups. With a hefty dose of poetic licence, I would like to tell you that I quoted accurately from *King Lear*, that Dad replied with something from Gandhi's memoirs or the Bhagavadgita. But this would be a lie. We ate in virtual silence, listening to the spool of nearby traffic, saying very little and certainly nothing profound or worth recording. I gave one of our two oranges to a passer-by. Dad eased down, made himself comfortable and closed his eyes. I ambled across to a group of nearby blue gums. They were decorated with shiny rectangular plaques (R114 – or should it have been R117?) made of cheap plastic. Some had fallen off and lay at the base of the tree. I read the names of the recently cremated, all written in the same hand in black koki. Raman Bhowan; Ramith Ramitheal; Sureshchindra Parbhoo; Harmigan Naidoo; Thakor Pemaramjee.

They were names now, nothing more – dead, just like my mum.

12

THE MELANCHOLY TURNPIKE: A TRAMPLE ALONG RECONCILIATION'S ROAD

The Voortrekker Monument to Freedom Park in Pretoria via Reconciliation Road — about three kilometres

On 16 December 2011, spooning through a gentle valley as it linked the Voortrekker Monument and Freedom Park, 'Reconciliation Road' was opened by 'his excellency Dr Jacob Zuma'. It was, press clippings told us at the time, 'part of the national project of reconciliation'. In less than four years, this wonderful initiative had been closed. The respective managements of the park and the monument were incapable of hammering out either a mutually respectful understanding or a working relationship for the sake of expedience. It was a contemporary version of what I had experienced in 'frontier country' during the walk that had taken Craig, Jako and me through the historical heartbeat of South Africa, the river bluffs and aloe-tall lands across which settlers and Xhosa pastoralists had *vloeked* and skirmished for close to a century. In Pretoria they simply closed things down. Both the Voortrekker Monument and Freedom Park had twin booms and little border-post-type brick cubicles in depressions on the edge of their property. With the closure, the booms had been lowered and the gates closed, traffic between the two reduced to a trickle. Like the border posts of Cold War East Berlin, you could not pass from the one to the other, which meant that, symbolically, you couldn't pass from the past into the present, or even – nostalgically, if you were walking in the opposite direction – from the present into the past. Without a foothold in the present, there was no firm ground from which to imagine the future, and without an imagined future we were unable to see the horizon, our present vague and leached of colour.

It didn't take much vision to see that the road's closure was a near-perfect metaphor for democracy's lack of progress. We were cast adrift in the land of Penny Sparrow, Juju and No. 1, the honorary doctor without a matric, stuck in a polit-ical and spiritual cul-de-sac. No one was talking, everyone was bitching, and not a week went by without the front pages being full of some crass demonstration of racist stupidity. Rhodes scholars were hung and quartered for examples of unadulterated racist misogyny, while young white fools took to social media to use the k-word. It was a freak show.

Discontent and fear of the future also took more subtle forms. My friends and class allies were hedging their bets and quietly squirrelling away cash offshore. Even my 79-year-old father, normally the most free-spirited and active of men, curious to a fault, had edged to the right. Over lasagne and green salad one recent Sunday, my wife, bless her, called him out on matters of race. As I watched and listened, wisely choosing not to take sides, she reminded him pointedly not to be intellectually crude. Generalisations in this racially overwrought atmosphere, she said a little sharply, were unwise. They were also wrong, particularly as so many black South Africans did the menial work that kept the country afloat – the petrol jockeys, the street-sweepers, the messengers and shelf packers.

Afterwards I couldn't help feel that the project of reconciliation was too burdened, asked to carry too much. It was not helped by a corrupt, inefficient faction of the ANC and their illegitimate leader or the failure in parts of the country to deliver not only houses, refuse collection and water but good, durable houses and regular clean water. Growing up in the suburbs in the 1980s, with high-school and university students still living at home, every so often you noticed the word 'apartheid' squashed onto stop signs. Now, spraypainted in quick white, was the word 'Zuma'. We had come so far but it sometimes seemed that we had travelled no distance at all.

Given this tragically laughable state of affairs, I was pleased to read earlier in 2016 that the respective parties on the hills overlooking Pretoria had patched up their differences and, well, reconciled, at least for the time being. The road was again open and with it came an opportunity too good to miss. My wife suggested that the book's concluding chapter should feature a walk of hope along Reconciliation Road. My dad chipped in that we should be sure to walk from the Voortrekker Monument to Freedom Park, from the past towards the present, in other words, and not the other way round. We set about inviting everyone I'd met in the course of writing the book to walk with us. We invited the Stirks and the Pringles from the Eastern Cape, Julian Pereira from Ixopo. I mailed Philip Kgosana, my walking companion from Makapanstad, land of Lutheran missions and tea parties in the afterlife. We would do the walk – it was a no-brainer – on Freedom Day, figuratively holding hands. It was roughly a year after I had started this book, with my walk from Orange Grove to Modderfontein. Like everyone else, we would be squinting slightly frantically into the future, wondering what it had in store.

The idea was one thing, its practical application quite another. Freedom Park is under the aegis of the Department of Arts and Culture, a state entity. By contrast, the Voortrekker Monument is a private concern set in rolling, valuable grounds, managed by a 14-strong council with a chairperson and a chief executive. Although it makes practical and commercial sense not only to keep the road open at all times, but also to yoke the two monuments closer together by issuing a single ticket allowing access to Freedom Park, the Voortrekker Monument and the road that links the two, this was an emotional bridge too far for the two management teams. As we investigated the logistics of the walk, we discovered that we'd have to buy separate tickets for each venue; if we wanted to gain access to the Voortrekker Monument at the main boom, it would cost R70 per person plus extra for cars and minibuses. The management of the Voortrekker Monument were, however, prepared to allow us entry for free if we came in through their booms on the

221

edge of their property on the Freedom Park side, and this is exactly what we eventually did. Heroically, Lisa liaised with the public-relations officers for each venue and although there was a sense in which they couldn't quite get their head around what we were proposing, they finally agreed, generously, to waive their entrance fees for the occasion. We took advantage of free entry to Freedom Park for the day and gathered in the empty Freedom Park parking lot. After Vuka Tshabalala's Orlando delegation finally arrived, we trooped in convoy down Reconciliation Road to a parking lot on the edge of the Voortrekker Monument's property, parked cars and minibuses and turned around to begin our walk. Vuka had brought along a group of children and several cynical old Soweto stalwarts, including the peerlessly irascible Bangomuzi Manyana. I recognised Bangomuzi immediately – we'd walked together in Soweto – and he was wearing an Orlando Pirates badge pinned delicately to his shirt pocket with a small gold safety pin. Craig and Jako had gunned up from Grahamstown in a *meneer* of a red bakkie the previous day, transporting Craig's ouma's furniture at the same time, and it was good to be united with Troepie and hear Craig's tales of student unrest on the Rhodes campus. So we set off, rambling down Reconciliation Road. It was a walk down the troubled turnpike of democracy.

Wednesday arrived overcast, with a vague threat of rain. Tuesday had been spent making coleslaw and chakalaka (a far more complicated process than I had realised, involving green peppers, masala and even baked beans) and, outside that night, over the darkened braai, I grilled wors. By the time the weather had cleared on Wednesday morning we were well prepared with cold food, lots to drink, paper plates and serviettes, plastic knives and forks. While the adults rambled, the children swarmed and ran. They played on the old farm equipment and machinery on the Voortrekker Monument's eastern side with endless energy. For them, this was not a monument to Afrikaner history and culture, a monument since segued into an icon of Afrikaner nationalism. Rather it was an outdoor theme park, somewhere where they could play and have fun, dance on bollards and jump in the sand. As the children swarmed ahead, we adults ambled along, chatting amiably. I can't speak for all of us, but I sensed there was much state-of-the-nation talk – with me there certainly was. As South Africans, we can't help ourselves. We live an identity that is foregrounded, between inverted commas: we are 'South Africans', rather than simply South Africans. Germans are only notionally Germans. This might be heightened at times of intense nationalism (while hosting a World Cup, for example) but other nations can go for weeks without thinking about who they are in a narrow, purely nationalistic sense. For South Africans, the fit is more wearying, less easy, for *who we are* is always troublesomely proximate to *what might happen*. This is a terrible position to occupy because we invariably reposition ourselves in relation to the latest news, as if there is no track record of, say, peacefulness and comparative economic prosperity behind us. If the rand plummets against the dollar, we get a headache; if the Springboks lose, we throw tantrums and sulk because we are – self-evidently – the worst team in the world; should JZ reach for the pre-municipal elections race card, we roll our eyes and predict a locust plague. It means that we're a nation perpetually on the verge of a nervous breakdown and it makes levity difficult, perspective impossible. Even our fun and thrill-seeking have that decadent, slightly destructive edge.

Maybe someday when we are older we will learn not to be so medieval. Not every sign is a portent. Some signs are simply empty, while only some carry meaning. For a nation with a shrinking Jewish community, we are, to use a Yiddish phrase, serial *kibitzers* – endless worriers at the petty beads of our existence.

So, our 20-strong procession walked, enjoying the sunshine and emptiness, the brush of wind across our cheeks, the feel of the freshly laid brick road under our feet. No one else had chosen to do what we were doing and we had reconciliation's road all to ourselves. The children streaked ahead, cartwheeling towards the first set of booms. When their group reached the border post they lined up across the road and saluted, a perfect foil to the situation's stern formalities. After the first post came an open area of no-man's-land where you walked along an underpass before you reached Freedom Park's booms. The guard was chilled as he chatted on his cellphone, barely batting an eyelid, and we crested up a slight incline, leaving the self-important theatricality of the border posts behind. Who would have believed it? The two parties couldn't man one post? It was as though the granite out of which the Voortrekker Monument was built had become a mentality. Or was it the other way round? Whatever the philosophy, the effect was the same. To meet it, Freedom Park needed to build a border post of their own. I wonder if the respective kings of national heritage considered passport control or visas. It was a space that spoke of power fantasies and rock-like control. Was it too much to hope for that one day this pseudo space, reminiscent of the Cold War, might be flattened altogether and you could walk through as South Africans, free, exchanging words and ideas. Sure, it was good to see the road open, the two parties talking; they were touching – or almost touching – but there was no embrace. Like so much else in contemporary South Africa, there was meeting but no connection.

Before long we had reached what Freedom Park guides call their *uitspanplek*, all sculptured lawns and ornamental thorn trees surrounded by soothing slate walls. We arranged food on a table and encouraged everyone to help themselves. Although the children hared around happily after they'd wolfed down their cold boerewors rolls and coleslaw, the conversation didn't lighten. People were thrilled to be where they were but they were worried, you could see it in their eyes. One of Vuka's mates predicted civil war within 50 years, an optimistic figure, some might have thought. Others bemoaned the callow youth, the generalised lack of respect. Bangomuzi and I shot the breeze under the meagre shade of a thorn tree, Bosman-style. He lives close to the Orlando Stadium, where the EFF's manifesto was about to be launched, and Juju – contemptuously referred to as '*that* woodworker' – was squarely on his mind. He was incandescent that UNISA could award him an honorary doctorate (although, in fact,

225

researching it afterwards, I discovered that Juju has simply earned an undergraduate degree). 'They must be a glorified high school, so help me God,' he growled. From education, Bangomuzi moved to his next target: the municipal elections. 'It's nonsense. Any non-entity can come out of his Zozo [hut] and declare himself a candidate,' he said. 'That's not politics, that's what makes a mockery of it all. Thabo, [Mbeki] he understood. Politics is all about economics because people can't eat your hot air – that's not going to feed and clothe you. He understood that. These non-entities are clueless.'

After continuing in this vein for some time, much of his invective well informed, all of it delivered with magnanimity and sweeping panache through a mouth without very many front teeth, Bangomuzi circled in on his prey. At this point we'd had a good 10 to 15 minutes of fulminating and railing, particularly but not exclusively about Julius Malema, but now it was time to dispense with the softening up, the thumps to the kidneys and heart. The haymaker came stealthily, with impressive speed, and was accompanied by an ever so slight shake of the head. 'The problem with Julius,' Bangomuzi said, as we all waited, straining forward, 'is that he's a hot-air bubbler.'

I couldn't stop laughing.

Over the coming days, I thought about Bangomuzi and his modes of oratory. He spoke well, with feeling and originality, a flourish or two of pure shebeen bullshit. Although he was the more natural showman, he reminded me a little of Kgosana. There was the same love of language, the same old-world eloquence, both coming from roughly the same period. It reminded me that America has Proclamation 118, otherwise known as the Thanksgiving Proclamation, the speeches of Abraham Lincoln and Thomas Jefferson, centuries of moving oration going back, in Lincoln's case, to what William Zinsser calls the 'harsh sonorities' of the King James Bible. Listening to Manyana's sprightly cadences, his cheeky worldview, brought home the fact that heritage encompasses more than run-down mills in the Eastern Cape and the Rissik Street post office. It also has to do with language – and how individuals and cultures express themselves in words. Manyana was chirpy and street-smart, knowing in the wearily sophisticated way of the experienced township habitué. It wasn't formal oratory as such, but it was certainly a style of thinking and talking, writing even, going back to *Drum* magazine and Can Themba – perhaps well beyond that. As the hot-air bubblers gained the offensive, so Bangomuzi and the Carling Black Label brigade would fade into insignificance, their style of thinking and speaking held only in the torpor of the occasional master's thesis. It was a shame, because Bangomuzi knows that the only way to stop the hot-air bubblers' advance is to go back to local idioms and forms. Against the broad front of populist demagoguery, of grotesquely ersatz ministers in their heels and twinsets, the cold fronts of vulgarity, South Africans have original words expressive of unique selves. They should build worlds with those words, as I have done here, allowing them to shine a light on all that is tepid and wrong. But there's more. So much has been forgotten in this society,

227

and so much more is being marginalised and forgotten in the very act of being officially remembered. Take James Mpanza and the women in the meander of the Klip River; take Philip Kgosana; take Thomas Pringle and Theopolis, the verities of the crusty Alan Paton. Take reconciliation's untrodden, hopelessly empty road.

To offset the bubbling, I have sought the commonality of that road, the kindness of strangers, the wisdom of the ramble. It is not much talked about any more, superseded as it is by the age of svelte digital novelties, the view from the sky and the speeding car window. For me, walking has opened up a new province, one of the land as well as the mind. It was a province that I suspected was there all along but one that became real only when I started to walk down magic roads and byways, wondering what I would see when I came out on the other side. What I found there was a lyric to South Africa – our new South Africa – a beautiful thing. In a very different context, Lincoln understood all this, for his country was similarly fractured and angry – so angry it went to war. He knew that the teeth of evil were lurking at the edge of the light, but this didn't mean that he was blind to the need for mercy and compassion – for gratitude. As he wrote in the Thanksgiving Proclamation of 1864, when the Civil War was nearing its end: 'It has pleased Almighty God to prolong our national life another year, defending us with His guardian care against unfriendly designs from abroad and vouchsafing to us in His mercy many and signal victories over the enemy, who is of our own household.'

Lincoln's words are beautiful and important. We would

do well to remind ourselves of them every so often, as he recommended the last Thursday of November every year be set aside as a day of thanksgiving and praise to God.

Luke Alfred is a veteran journalist and well-known author. He currently works as a freelance journalist in Johannesburg for a variety of local and international publications and websites. He worked at the *Sunday Times* for 10 years (just under four as sports editor) and the *Sunday Independent* for nearly seven. In a freelance capacity, he currently works regularly for the *Financial Mail*, *Cricinfo* and the *Mail and Guardian*.

This is his fifth book of non-fiction – and his first of travel writing, autobiography and history. His previous four books were all on a sporting theme, the most-recent of which was the story of the 1974 British Lions rugby tour of South Africa, *When the Lions came to Town*.

He is happily married to Lisa and they have three sons, two Labradors, two cats and a large vegetable garden. They have also recently been visited by a Spotted Eagle Owl. They are hoping she will nest in their garden.

ACKNOWLEDGEMENTS

I adventured far and wide in the preparation of this book, and there are a great many people to thank and recognise. Firstly, then, to those who specifically asked me not to name them for fear of reprisals or violence (they know who they are), thank you for your Friday-night generosity, your yarns and the mapping out of your precious world.

Then, to those who allowed me to walk on their land or housed me and friends, or both. My gratitude to Colin and Lyn Stirk of Southwell, and to Howson Long for finding and showing us Theopolis. Alex, Barrie and David Pringle were remarkably trusting and open-hearted, allowing Craig Paterson and me to spend a night in their home after walking on their farm in Thomas Pringle country. A word of gratitude, too, to Ernest Pringle, who showed us his private museum. I didn't realise it at the time but it was a memorable morning. Thank you as well to Craig, a fine companion on three of my walks, and Jako Bezuidenhout, storyteller extraordinaire, on two of them.

My deep thanks, also, to 'the hillbilly', Julian Pereira, and Cheryl Biggs, owner of King's Grant in Ixopo, Pippa Cope of the Tara Rokpa Centre in the Marico, Sandra van Bart, Philip 'Kortbroek' Kgosana, and Vuka Gladstone Tshabalala and his

Orlando friends, particularly Bangomuzi Manyana. I won't forget you guys in a hurry.

I was also helped in a variety of small ways by librarians, heritage fundis, museum curators and public-relations and communication officers. At Modderfontein, Peet Hattingh walked me round the graveyard, while Mari Gravett arranged it all. Martie Smith was helpful in the Modderfontein Museum, where I spent an interesting morning. I was helped, too, on different occasions by Laddy Mckechnie at the National Library in Cape Town, and by Margaret Constant at the Simon's Town Historical Society Library. Thanks must also go to the staff of the Cory Library at Rhodes, in Grahamstown, where I spent several snatched hours of reading and note-taking.

James Ball of the Heritage Portal was always at hand to help or answer a query, and John Perlman put me onto the remarkable story of Philip Kgosana. Nice one, John. Magda Strydom, the event coordinator at Freedom Park, was incredibly accommodating in helping us to arrange the Reconciliation Road walk, as was her colleague on the Voortrekker Monument side, Erna Erasmus. You both made our 'Freedom Day' walk a special day. Cheers.

A heartfelt thank-you, too, to Annie Olivier, formerly of Tafelberg, for taking on the idea of this book with openness and affection. Thank you also to Maryna Lamprecht, for seeing the project through to conclusion and Mark Ronan for his light and careful editing.

Finally, thanks to my wife, Lisa, for her love and blessing.

NOTES AND REFERENCES

Introduction

The quotation from Dickens is from 'Night Walks' in Charles Dickens, *The Uncommercial Traveller*. Heron Books, 1970, page 149 (originally published 1875).

Camilo José Cela, *Journey to the Alcarria*. Cambridge: Granta Books, 1990, page 5.

Chapter 2

The 'infantile proletarianism' quote is taken from John Berger and Timothy Neat's 1989 film, *Play Me Something*, a joint British Film Institute/Channel 4 production.

Ben Maclennan, *Glenmore: The Story of a Forced Removal*. Johannesburg: South African Institute of Race Relations, 1987, pages 65, 67, 68.

Doris Stirk, *Southwell Settlers*. Privately published, first edition 1971, pages 10, 37.

Chapter 3

The quote 'We were pilgrims in the savage wilds of Africa' is taken from Randolph Vigne, *Thomas Pringle: South African Pioneer, Poet and Abolitionist*. Oxford: James Currey, 2012, page 74.

Thomas Pringle, *Some Account of the Present State of the*

English Settlers in Albany, South Africa. Printed for T.G. Underwood, London, 1824, pages 6, 11.

Ralph Waldo Emerson, *Nature and Selected Essays*. London and New York: Penguin Classics, 2003, page 175.

Chapter 4
Alan Paton, *Cry, the Beloved Country: A Story of Comfort in Desolation*. London: Jonathan Cape, 1948, page 20.

Chapter 5
Catherine Knox and Cora Coetzee, *Victorian Life at the Cape 1870–1900*. Simon's Town: Fernwood Press, 1992, page 163.

Yuval Noah Harari, *Sapiens: A Brief History of Humankind*. London: Vintage, 2011, page 396.

For the press quotes relating to Zuma's decision to fire Nene, see Anton Harber, 'The Week Zuma's Armour was Penetrated', *Business Day*, 17 December 2015; Steven Friedman, 'Thwarted Attack Reins In the ANC's Rural Barons', *Business Day*, 17 December 2015; Rian Malan, *Daily Maverick*, http://firstthing.dailymaverick.co.za/article?id=73228#. V1VH9NJ97IU.

Chapter 7
Joseph Lelyveld, *Move Your Shadow: South Africa, Black and White*. London: Michael Joseph, 1986, page 317.

Chapter 8
Report on the Feasibility of Table Mountain Dams by Thomas Stewart to the Corporation of Cape Town, 1898. File in the National Library of South Africa, Cape Town.

Chapter 9

Olive Nieuwoudt, *My Cederberg Story*. Private publication by Susan de la Bat (Nieuwoudt), Durbanville, 2015, pages 109, 124, 166.

Stephen Watson, *A Writer's Diary*. Cape Town: Queillerie, 1997, pages 47, 61, 76, 77.

Chapter 10

Herman Charles Bosman, 'Marico Revisited' in *Bosman at his Best: A Choice of Stories and Sketches*. Cape Town and Pretoria: Human & Rousseau, 1965, page 128.

For the Rinpoche obituary, see Vishvapani Blomfield, *The Guardian*, 20 October 2013, http://www.theguardian.com/world/2013/oct/20/choje-akong-tulku-rinpoche.

Chapter 11

Eric Itzkin, *Gandhi's Johannesburg: Birthplace of Satyagraha*. Johannesburg: Wits University Press in association with Museum Africa, 2000, page 5.

Chapter 12

William Zinsser, *On Writing Well: An Informal Guide to Writing Nonfiction*. New York: HarperCollins, 1990, page 130.

INDEX

African National Congress
(ANC) 125, 140, 147, 220
Alexandra Dam (Table Moun-
tain) 155, 158, 163, 166
Alfred, Jake 169–186
Alfred, Mike (Dad) 18–19, 30,
204–220
Alfred, Samuel 169–186
Alfred, Thomas 67
Algeria 171, 173, 175–176
Apartheid 21, 44, 108, 210, 220
Avigliana (Italy) 25, 33
Baines, Thomas 71–72, 80
Barker, Reverend George 55–57
Barker, Tom 74
Beresford, David 118
Berger, John 40, 185
Bezuidenhout, Jako 37–58,
218, 222, 235
Boer War 163, 192, 209
Bosman, Herman Charles
187–201
Botha, General Louis 209
Boyhood (Richard Linklater
movie) 182
Brilliant 60–62
Brixton Cemetery 202,
211–212

Bunhill Fields (Islington,
London) 74–75
Butler, Guy 185
Carisbrooke siding 81–98
Carlin, John 118
Cartuccere (cartridge girls) 25,
33
Cederberg 169–186
Cela, Camilo José 9
Chaucer, Geoffrey 150
Clovelly Station 103–104
Coetzee, J.M. 95
Credo Mutwa Centre 133–136
Cry, the Beloved Country (Alan
Paton) 81–98, 124
Daily Maverick (website) 116, 120
De Beers 190–191
De Villiers Dam (Table
Mountain) 154–155, 157, 163
Dickens, Charles 9
Dido Valley Cemetery 109–111
Dodds, William 63
Du Val, Charles 207
Eastern Cape Herald 72
Eikeboom 171, 176
Eildon Farm 59–80
Fairbairn, John 76
Fenton, Blanche 206–207

Fish Hoek 99–120
Foster, Maurice 21–22
Freedom Park 218–229
Friedman, Steven 115–116
Frontier Wars *("Kaffir Wars")* 43
Gandhi, Mahatma 138, 202–217
Garskraal 173
Glencairn Beach 105–109
Glenmore 44–47, 49
Gordhan, Pravin 99, 116
Gordimer, Nadine 117
Grahamstown 40–61, 65, 74, 79, 222
Gray, William 54, 56–57
Grocott's Mail (Grahamstown) 40, 45
Groot Marico 187–201
Guardian (newspaper) 118
Hamidia Mosque 205
Harari, Yuval Noah 114–115
Harber, Anton 115
Hattingh, Peet 33–34
Hely-Hutchinson Dam (Table Mountain) 155, 159–160, 162, 163, 166
Hindu Crematorium, Brixton Cemetery 183, 202–203, 212–213
HMS Brilliant 60–62
Hole in the Wall, Transkei 19
Hope Road, Mountain View 11
Hunt, Henry 68–69
'In the Withaak's Shade'

(Herman Charles Bosman) 194
Independent (newspaper) 118
Ixopo 81–98, 221, 235
Jabula Recreation Centre and Library 16, 18, 22, 25
Jacobson, Dan 95
Kalk Bay 99–120
Kallenbach, Hermann 138, 202, 204
Kariega River 42, 44
Karoo Morning (Guy Butler) 185
Kasteelpoort Aerial Cableway 161–163
Kgosana, Phillip Ata 139–151, 221, 228
Kimmerling, Albert 13–15, 26
Krause, Fritz 208–209
Kromrivier 173, 175, 176–177
Kruger, Paul 209
Kundera, Milan 126
Larkin, Philip 177
Lawrence, Weschler 184
Lelyveld, Joseph 140, 144–149
Lemoen Plaas (became Orange Grove) 27, 28
Lincoln, Abraham 227–228
Linklater, Richard 182
Linksfield Ridge 12, 15
Lloyd Webber, Andrew 83
Louis Botha Avenue 11–27
Lyhne, Lisa 84–88, 181–183, 193, 219, 222, 237

Lyndhurst 16, 20, 30

Maclennan, Ben 46–48

Mafani, Ben 45–46

Mail & Guardian (newspaper) 122

Makapanstad 138–151

Makapanstad Lutheran Church 145–146

Malan, Rian 116–120

Malema, Julius (Juju) 219, 226

Manyana, Bangomuzi 222, 227, 236

Marico Eye 187–201

Marr-Scott, Skye 169–186

Mbeki, Thabo 226

McDougal, Brett 28

Mehliss, Dr John 'Max' ('Dr Mielies') 24

Modderfontein Dynamite Factory 30–32, 203

Moisant, John 14

Molteno Reservoir 156

Mostert, Noel 43

Mountain View 11–27

Mpanza, James 'Sofasonke' 122–137, 228

Muizenberg 99–120

Mutwa, Credo 133–136

My Cederberg Story (Olive Nieuwoudt) 173–174, 176–177

My Traitor's Heart (Rian Malan) 116–120

Nahoon Racetrack 13

Nene, Nhlanhla 99, 115

New York Times (newspaper) 140

New Yorker (magazine) 116, 184

Nieuwoudt, Olive 173–174, 176–177

Niewoudts of Dwarsrivier 173–174, 176–177

Nové Zámky 25

Olivier, Annie and Jacques 222, 236

Oppenheimer, Sir Ernest 133–135

Orange Grove 14, 25–28

Oriental Plaza 207–208

Orlando (Soweto) 123–125, 134, 147, 222, 225, 236

Orlando Pirates Football Club 124, 222

Paterson, Craig 37–59, 64–65, 71, 77, 218, 222, 235

Paton, Alan 77, 81–98, 228

Paton's Country Railway 81–98

Pereira, Julian 81–98, 221, 235

Phillips, James 119

Player, Ian 18

Prijepolje (Serbian town) 85

Prince, Mary 64–65, 76

Pringle, Alex, Barrie and David 62–76, 221

Pringle, Ernest 77–80, 235

Pringle, Robert 63
Pringle, Thomas 57, 59–80,
    122, 228
Rand Daily Mail 14
Reconciliation Road 218–229
Rhodes University 37, 59
Rhodes, Cecil John 100, 113
Rietfontein Infectious Diseases
    Hospital 23, 28
Rinpoche, Akong 198–200
Salem 35–58
Sanddrif 169–186
Sandringham 22, 23
Schlebusch (near Cologne) 25
Schlesinger, Isidore 211
Searelle, Luscombe 206–207,
    210
Sederhoutkloof 172, 180
Simon's Town 99–120
Simon's Town Historical
    Society 109, 112, 115, 236
Smuts, Jan 19, 209
Sobukwe, Robert 139–140,
    147–148
Somerset, Lord Charles 76, 101
South African Institute of Race
    Relations 47, 139
Southwell 35–58
Southwell Club 38, 52, 53
Soweto 121–137, 222
St James 99–120
St James's Church,
    Southwell 53

Stainton siding 81–98
Stevenson, Robert Louis 9
Stewart, Thomas 157, 159,
    161–163, 167
Stirk, Colin, Lyn and Lynn
    50–53, 56, 57, 221
Stirk, Doris 53–55
Sydenham Hill 13, 26
Table Mountain 152–168
Tara Rokpa Buddhist Retreat
    191–201, 216, 235
The Book of Laughter and Forgetting
    (Milan Kundera) 126
The Canterbury Tales (Geoffrey
    Chaucer) 150
Theopolis (Mission Station) 37,
    55–57, 228, 235
Thompson, E.P. 136
Tierhok Farm 172
Tolstoy Farm, south of
    Lenasia 138
Tolstoy, Leo 20, 138
Tshabalala, Vuka Gladstone
    122–137, 222, 225
Uitkyk Pass, Cederberg 175
University of Cape Town 139,
    181
Van Bart, Egbert 189, 197
Van Niekerk, Marlene 95
Van Onselen, Charles 43
Van Rooyen, David (Des) 99
Vanity Fair (magazine) 117
Vansittart, Nicholas 69

Victoria Dam (Table Mountain) 155, 158, 163, 166
Vilakazi Street (Soweto) 127, 129, 131
Voortrekker Monument 218–229
Watson, Stephen 77, 177–186
Witgat tree, on Pringle land 63, 80
Woodhead Dam (Table Mountain) 155, 156, 159–162, 166
Woodhead Tunnel (Table Mountain) 155–157
Woodstock 142–143, 146, 177
Wool price, spike in 1950s 73–74
Zinsser, William 227
Zuma, Jacob 99, 115–116, 218, 220, 224